WALK WITH
—— *the* ——
SHADOW

In memory of my beloved
husband Sal,

In God's Love,
Marie

Thank you for your support.
May all the blessings of
life be with you & Yours,

In His Name,
Marie E. Bouchard

WALK WITH

—— *the* ——

SHADOW

VAL & MARIE BOUCHARD

COMPILED BY TERRY M. GEASLIN

TATE PUBLISHING & Enterprises

Scripture taken from The Jerusalem Bible, copyright © 1966 by Darton, Longman & Todd, Ltd. and Doubleday, a division of Bantam Doubleday Dell Publishing Group, Inc. Reprinted by permission.

The opinions expressed by the author are not necessarily those of Tate Publishing, LLC.

Published by Tate Publishing & Enterprises, LLC
127 E. Trade Center Terrace | Mustang, Oklahoma 73064 USA
1.888.361.9473 | www.tatepublishing.com

Tate Publishing is committed to excellence in the publishing industry. The company reflects the philosophy established by the founders, based on Psalm 68:11,
"The Lord gave the word and great was the company of those who published it."

Book design copyright © 2010 by Tate Publishing, LLC. All rights reserved.
Cover design by Tyler Evans
Interior design by Lynly D. Grider

Published in the United States of America

ISBN: 978-1-61663-309-7
1. Biography & Autobiography / Personal Memoirs
2. Health & Fitness / Diseases / Heart

10.04.26

DEDICATION

To my beloved husband, Val. We traveled this glorious path with each other's love and support. Even though your physical presence is no longer here, when we needed your guidance in completing this book, you were with us and we felt it.

Terry and Connie of the Living Years, thank you for your gift in transforming all of our many writings (letters, documents, messages, jotted notes) and photos into the book I visualized so many years ago.

ACKNOWLEDGMENTS

My heartfelt gratitude goes out to so many for all of the love, prayers, and support during very difficult times. Thank you seems inadequate. What I feel in my heart is immeasurable. Each one of you has left an indelible memory that I treasure and will keep in my heart and mind for all time. Love, the ultimate gift, leaves me with humbling grace.

To the medical professionals and hospitals, you utilized your God-given talents above and beyond expectations. I could not have asked for more. God has allowed the advancement of technology and modern medicine, giving men and women the knowledge and skill to accomplish the unimaginable.

To everyone (family, friends and those whom we do not know) who lifted us up in prayers, you are precious gifts indeed. God listened. His mercy endured beyond imagination.

To the donor family, I want to express appreciation for sharing your loved one with us. It was not in vain. Val believed God was working through him. It was always "Yes, my Lord" until the mission was complete and there was time to rest for my beloved.

God is hope, and this story says so much about hope. I praise God for all of you and will forever hold you in my prayers and heart. You are a blueprint in my mind.

How could I ever forget you? I was given a precious gift: my beloved husband for another happy quality of life for twenty-two years and three months. Amazing!

Prayers and love to you and yours,

Marie E. Bouchard

TABLE OF CONTENTS

PREFACE

This book has a three-fold purpose: to tell a true story about faith, to show the good that can come from the organ donor program, but most importantly, to glorify Him in whom we live and move and have our being.

This is a story of miracles.

A miracle, defined by *Webster's Dictionary*, is "an extraordinary event manifesting divine intervention in human affairs." The word *miracle*, like *love, faith, loyalty*, and *honor* has become devalued by overuse—uses for occurrences that are not truly the intervention of the supernatural but merely events that amaze us or perhaps mildly surprise us. A true miracle is the hand of God laid upon his creation.

This is also the story of a journey into unknown territory with a Master Guide second to none. The path traverses many peaks and valleys, taxing emotions to the very core in our being. Only with God's divine grace have we persevered.

EULOGY

Valmore Frances Bouchard
8–13–1928 / 7–4-1990 / 10–30–2006

Val (photo by Ruth Carey)

Be the best you can be. Sounds like a recruiting slogan for the army or the marines, but is not. These were the words of a dying father to his nine-year-old son, Val. These words then became the motto for the young son for his whole life in whatever he was doing.

Enlisting in the navy at the age of seventeen, he served in World War II submarines for nine years and then was sent for shore duty in Los Angeles as a naval recruiter. In 1955, Val was selected to participate in the development and training for the start-up of Admiral Rickover's Navy Nuclear Program. For the next ten years, he was responsible for the submarine's engineering force in all its phases from monitoring, construction, training, testing systems, and the actual operations of this nuclear sub. He retired from the navy in 1965.

After retiring, he began working for General Dynamic in Boston, Massachusetts, in the Shipyard Nuclear Division as a Senior Nuclear Test Engineer. After three years working there, he became employed at the Yankee Atomic Engineering office in Boston. A year and a half later, he was transferred to the Vermont Yankee Nuclear Power Plant for construction and start-up. Here he functioned as the technical operations manager for nine years. Seeing no advancement in his future, Val quit that position and became vice president and technical manager of Vikem Industries and was the decontamination and restoration manager at Three Mile Island. This was after the March 1979 incident. Being asked by Bechtel numerous times to become part of their team, he did so and became a traveling expert and troubleshooter in the nuclear field achieving worldwide recognition for his accomplishments.

In 1984, Val suffered his first major heart attack and afterward had a six-way heart bypass. Not letting this deter him, he was soon back to volunteering and doing all he could for his church, the school, and Knights of Columbus projects. His condition deteriorated in 1990, and on July 4, he was the recipient of a new heart at Vanderbilt Hospital by the well-known surgeon Dr. William Frist, who is our Senate majority leader.

Married for forty-nine years and just short of their fiftieth anniversary on the twenty-sixth of November, Val and Marie were two peas in a pod that complimented each other in everything they did, raising two great sons, Val Jr. and Jim, and because of circumstances, adopted and raised two grandchildren, Chris and Christine.

I became acquainted with the Bouchards when I was transferred back to Knoxville in 1988. Even though living in Knoxville, I decided to make St. Mary's my parish. In 1989, I joined the Knights of Columbus, and at every event, which entailed serving of food, you could find Val and his whole family working on the project and, in most cases, spearheading the entire affair. In the late fall of 1995, our assistant pastor came to the Knights of Columbus meeting and told us of the deplorable condition that a neighboring family was living in and asked if the Knights would be willing to get involved and help the family. As it turned out, the family that Father was referring to was our own Dominican Sisters and the deplorable conditions of the convent. After sending in a team of Knights to assess the needs, it soon became apparent that the Knights were way over their heads in what was needed and the funds that it would take to do the job.

Val sprang into action and got the word out to parishioners and his other contacts about the needs of the convent. Working in whatever free time he could manage and for numerous hours at night, after he got off from work at his job, you could find Val and Marie, plus other family members, for over a year working on the convent restoration. Upon completion of the renovations to the convent in the spring of 1997, over $70,000 worth of renovations and thousands of hours of work were done on the convent through generosity of individual parishioners, Knights, and the contacts of Val and Marie Bouchard. Also not known but by few, many, many times funds for what was needed at the time came out of the pockets of Val himself. He wanted the best of what could be provided for the Sisters.

In 1999, the visions of another Knight, Deacon Carl Wust, were presented to our Knights of Columbus Council to build on the church grounds a memorial for all the babies killed by abortion and a place where people affected by abortions could come and pray. Before he could see this vision become a reality, Deacon Wust passed away but left in his will funds available to start up his project.

The Knights then formed a committee to undertake the building of this memorial, which would be called the Angel Garden. While there were many Knights who initially helped on this project, it was Val whose own vision made the project a reality and who, over the years with the help of family members, has seen to the improvements and upkeep of the Angel Garden.

In 2002, at the Knights of Columbus State Convention held in Knoxville, Val and Marie Bouchard and their family were chosen as the Knights of Columbus State of Tennessee Family of the Year.

I have had the privilege of having numerous conversations with Val over the years and was always impressed with his knowledge, insight, and caring for others. His great wit and humor always got me laughing and feeling good. He was a great mentor to me. He was very proud of all of his children and grandchildren—always bragging on them at every chance he got, but never looking for personal glory. He has instilled in each of his children and grandchildren his own work ethics of doing your best, going the extra mile and always giving back.

Val believed that whatever good he accomplished, it was God that was working through him to accomplish the mission. It was impossible to sum up in any short synopsis all the good things and kindness that Val has done in his life. In fact, he probably has done more volunteer and charitable work since his rebirth sixteen years ago with the implant of his new heart than most people do in their entire lifetimes.

I know that on Monday morning, October 30 at 7:00 a.m., my mother was one of many welcoming Val to heaven and thanking him again for all the kindness that he had shown to her and to me.

On most people's grave markers, you will see their birth date-dash, dash, dash, and then their date of death. Not really important is the date of birth nor the date of death, but the life that the dashes represent. In Val's situation, you could see 8/13/1928 date of birth-dash, dash, dash 7/4/1990 date of rebirth with a new heart-dash, dash, dash 10/30/2006 date of rebirth into eternal life.

With the welcoming words of two Fathers, saying, "Welcome Val, my beloved son, come and rest, suffer no more. *You have been the best you could be* as a Christian, as a son, as a husband, as a father, as a grandfather, as a brother, as a boss, as a coworker, as a mentor, and as a friend." We'll miss you, dear friend, but will never forget you. Be looking forward to our reunion someday. You are forever in my heart and prayers. Please remember me in yours. Vivat Jesus, Bill.

ON THE MOVE

Home in the Basin

Fall of 1969 - After twenty years in the military, my husband, Val, took employment in a quaint little town in southern Vermont. Val had always dreamed of building his own home, and after an exhausting search, we acquired a piece of mountaintop property with a breathtaking sixty-mile view of land known as the Basin.

Only one couple lived there at the time. The woman wrote a weekly column for the local newspaper about life down on the farm, titled "Hilltop Housewife." She let it be known we were not exactly welcome on her mountain. I was shy and thin-skinned, and this made me feel very uncomfortable. Val, on the other hand, did not care what Hilltop Housewife thought because he has always approached every project with a positive attitude. Two words that did not exist in his vocabulary were *can't* and *no*. He heard them as *can* and *yes*! His positive attitude and reassurances, however, were not enough to still the reluctance I kept concealed deep inside.

In my simple way of thinking, just because Val had built a garage once did not qualify him as a master builder. The garage did turn out great, but what would a house look like? Even though I remained reluctant—or more so scared to death—I kept my apprehensions silent and outwardly supported him.

Our home was nearly completed and landscaped by the fall of 1970. In spite of my misgivings and fears, it was beautiful both inside and out. I was so happy, and now we could enjoy the fruits of our labor. For Val and me, it was our Utopia. Val taught me what can be accomplished with an attitude that won't say no—along with bruised fingers and scraped knees! The home was our dream fulfilled.

I was comfortable too. After December 16, 1970, the Hilltop Housewife column publicly welcomed us to the mountain by telling of our labor and saying what good neighbors we had turned out to be.

Marie with Dick

One night, when Val was collecting for the cancer fund, he met a seventy-five-year-old man, Dick, who had undergone surgery and was all alone. Val asked me to make some soup to take him. I did, and this was the beginning of a wonderful friendship. When his failing eyesight made it impossible for him to drive anymore, I became his chauffeur. I helped him make a necessary move from his home to a retirement center. He never wanted a television, but I convinced him to get one with headphones so the volume wouldn't bother the other residents of the center. Sometimes when I visited him, I caught him laughing at the comedy programs, so I knew he enjoyed the television although he pretended he didn't need it at all.

In the summer of 1979, Val went to Three Mile Island in Pennsylvania to assist in the cleanup after the accident at the power plant. Our youngest son, Jim, was going into his senior year in high school, so he and I remained in Vermont for him to finish school there. Whenever I got lonely for Val, I made the eight-hour drive to visit him. He was working long hours, seven days a week, and could not make the trip home.

When the assignment at Three-Mile Island had finished, Val came home and just rested several weeks before deciding to take a job offer with a company he had worked with at Three-Mile Island. The job would take him back to the town we lived in before moving to our mountain in Vermont, about a two-hour commute away.

Val rented a nice apartment and came home on weekends. I usually went to visit him one day a week when the weather was nice. Val was working long hours but was very happy.

A chain of events began to happen that put the two of us on a fast-moving train. In the spring of 1983, a decision was made to sell our home. In the fall, Jim would be going to college, and Val didn't want me on the mountain alone. Neither did we want to leave the house unoccupied while I joined Val in the apartment. Reluctantly, we agreed to place the house on the market. The maintenance of this property had grown difficult for us, especially during the harsh winters. We spent thirteen beautiful years in the home we had built together, but it was time for a change.

The house sold in a strange way, especially for that remote location in the Basin. Over the years, a few other homes were built on the mountain. We notified our neighbors and planned to talk with a real estate agent. One of the neighbors had his house on the market for over two years, so we felt it would be a long time before our house would sell.

However, even before we could call an agent, I returned

home one day to find a note on the door which indicated a name and telephone number of people who were interested in the house. I arranged for them to come and see the inside of our home. They looked around the house for approximately twenty minutes, told me the house was lovely, and left. Since Val was out of town working, I had to communicate with him via telephone. A week later, they called, arranging to meet for dinner with Val and me to discuss the purchase and sale of our home. By the end of the meal, we had a sales agreement along with a large down payment. There was no financing to be involved because they would be paying cash for the purchase. Val said we would need until September to have everything ready and be out of the house. The buyers said that was fine but asked if they could bring a few things to store in the garage. I said that would be fine, and soon the garage was full of their belongings to be moved into the house. Val and I did not know it would be nearly the entire contents of their home, from which they were moving. This made me anxious and caused me to work much faster than I'd planned, and we were ready to move out of our home by July 3.

It took a long time for us to be accepted when we first moved to Vermont, but we had made friends, and it was very hard to leave. On July 4, 1983, we took our last walk through the house that had been home for thirteen years. It was difficult to contain the tears as we looked at all we were leaving behind. We tried to capture all the good memories to keep with us. We left a bottle of champagne on their kitchen table, which we placed where our table once stood, along with two glasses and a card wishing them as much happiness as we had in the house that was to be their new home.

We began looking for land for a new home. Val's apartment was nice but small, and I missed my flower gardens. We found a ten-acre parcel that was part of a working apple orchard. In exchange for the fruit, the present owners would continue to tend the trees after we bought the land. I had always dreamed of living in an orchard. As a young girl, I had picked apple blossoms for my mother, who would put them in a bowl on the table and smile, saying how good they made the house smell.

We put a clothes line on our new home site, and I would hang our sheets there so they would smell fresh from the wind through the apple trees. As I waited for the laundry to dry, I would look at the stone walls and dream about the house we were planning. But that dream was not to become reality. Val made a career change, which took us out of New England all together—all the way to Tennessee.

We found a house in Oak Ridge, Tennessee, and I returned to New England to finalize our matters there. I stayed with Jim in his apartment where he was attending college at that time. There seemed to be no time to accomplish all I needed to do, but my trust was in the Lord, and he carried me through all the arduous tasks involved in making this move.

After I finished arrangements for our move, I managed to spend a day with Dick. Our discussion centered on God and my feelings about a personal knowledge of him. Dick, however, was agnostic and believed that whatever this

Supreme Being was, there had to be so much more than the God whom I believed in.

I was deeply concerned that Dick did not want to accept the invitation to know God personally, to have God as his personal Savior so I could have the hope of his friendship throughout eternity. Dick was not of a demonstrative nature, but he hugged me for a long time and told me I had meant everything to him, like a daughter he never had. He was very proud of Val's career and accomplishment and understood that our moving was necessary. Before I left, Dick and I set a date for me to return to Vermont in June so we could plant a tree together on his former property, which he dearly loved. Little did I know the disaster that lay ahead of me that would prevent me from keeping our date.

It was a cold, damp, dreary day in February 1984 as I flew out of Bradley International Airport in Connecticut. Tennessee was beautiful with its spring-like weather. What a contrast to that of the North. On March 1, 1984, we closed on the house in Oak Ridge.

The next several weeks were consumed with choosing wallpaper and fabrics to give our new home the taste of our personalities instead of those of the previous owners. The backyard was being prepared for installation of an in-ground swimming pool. Everything seemed to dovetail well, and by summer, we would be settled in our new home and could begin to enjoy our new surroundings.

LITTLE DID WE KNOW

Val, May 17, 1984 (photo by Ruth Carey)

May 1984 - Val was almost totally consumed with his work and had to travel to Plymouth, Massachusetts, for a project that would take about a month to complete. After some time, Val was able to come home, but for only one day to have his photograph taken for the corporation's newsletter so it would make a printing deadline.

While he was home, he convinced me to join him in Plymouth to take some time off to enjoy myself and to spend some time with him. I was in the middle of the redecorating and the pool installation and felt I needed to be in Oak Ridge. But Val changed my mind, and, of course,

I went. As I look back, I see it was God's plan for me to go with Val.

He said the tourist season hadn't started yet, and I could enjoy spring all over again in the quaint little town. Our room overlooked the bay where the replica of the Mayflower harbored. Val and I enjoyed the quaint historic village of Plymouth for just over a week before our nightmare began.

During the day, Val seemed to tire easy, and he found excuses of blaming his total involvement on the project and hurrying to have it ready so he could return home. As days went by, Val grew more tired with the least amount of physical effort, such as walking to and from areas of relatively short distances. The stairs seemed harder to climb, and he would be completely exhausted after going up just twenty steps. He found himself having to stop and rest every seven or eight steps to allow his "heartburn" to go away.

Never having been sick or in the hospital, Val considered himself to be in good health although he wasn't knowledgeable enough about the warning signals of his health. His enthusiasm with the project had his mind thinking at night, and he honestly believed that most of us have been in his situation more than once. When the adrenaline flows, we seem to not listen to what our body is telling us. He, of all people, should have known something about better health but confessed he was completely ignorant. He would also use his diet as an excuse and easily justified the cause as restaurant food—true self-denial.

On May 30, we went to dinner at an Italian restaurant. Val was very quiet that evening, and I attributed it to fatigue and the fact that he had a lot on his mind because the project he had set up was now being turned over to the next stage in the operation. We would soon be returning to Tennessee.

When retiring to bed for the evening, Val complained of having indigestion. I placed my hand on his back and rubbed between his shoulder blades in order to relieve the discomfort. He asked me to stop almost immediately because he could not tolerate the motion of my hand on his back. It made him nauseous and increased his discomfort, providing him with no relief. I suggested that Val should see a doctor, but he said he would probably feel better with some rest. I said, "I think you are having a heart attack." Val responded that he was not having any of the symptoms one is supposed to have when experiencing a heart attack. He was referring to pain in the arm and pain in the chest. His pain, he explained, was attributed to the rich and spicy foods he had eaten at dinner.

We fell asleep shortly afterwards. I awoke at 6:00 a.m. and realized Val was not there and assumed he went to work. That was not unusual for him since he often went to work at that hour of the day and would let me sleep. I remember feeling uneasy that particular morning and couldn't go back to sleep. So I had a lazy morning reading until about nine and decided to take a bath. While in the tub, I heard a loud knock at the hotel door. I grabbed a towel and wrapped it around me to answer the door. When I asked who's there, Val responded, "It's me, honey." I opened the door for him and asked him if he was feeling any better. He replied that he was just coming from the drugstore.

The druggist had suggested Riopan, and if that did not help him, he should see a doctor. Val said he had taken the medication and it had given him some relief. I still thought he should see a doctor, but Val told me he wanted to wait until we returned to Oak Ridge in a couple of days. It was raining outside, and he came back to the hotel to see me and give me the option of having the vehicle for the day while he went back to work. He had been to breakfast with coworkers and could go back to the plant with them, leaving me the car. I decided to venture out without any idea of where I would go or what I would do while out driving around.

I did some shopping that day, but could not keep my mind off Val. I asked myself, *Do I have any real cause to be so concerned?* I had a very uneasy feeling about Val, but I decided to browse and ended up in a jewelry store. For many years, I had looked for a cross pendant but could never find one I really liked. That day I found a cross pendant, and after much debate with myself, I was convinced that it would look terrific around my neck. I am someone who is not attracted to material things, so I felt guilty for buying an item so expensive for myself, but the guilt was short lived. I walked out of the store wearing the cross pendant. I was completely unaware of the amount of time I spent in the jewelry store and realized it was time to pick Val up from work.

It was still raining when Val got to the car, and immediately I noticed his labored breathing. I mentioned my concern to him, but Val rationalized it was because he hurried in the rain and that he might be just a little out of shape. In an effort to take the focus away from the concern I had for Val, I told him he bought me an expensive gift that day and showed him the beautiful cross. He replied, "It's beautiful, and I'm glad. You waited a long time to find the cross you wanted."

Val asked me if I was hungry and if I would like to have dinner before going to the hotel. He indicated he would only eat lightly since he was not hungry. I said, "Let's go to the hotel first to freshen up before going out." I was trying not to alarm him with my concern, and he agreed to my suggestion.

It took him a long time to get up to the room, which was only one flight of stairs. I assumed he stopped and talked with someone on his way to our room. He was always friendly, and Val could easily find a friend for life. Once he arrived at the room, he took a shower, lay down for a rest, and went to sleep. He awoke abruptly after a thirty-minute nap and asked the time. I told him it was six thirty, and he reaffirmed the idea of getting me something to eat. Val started to get dressed, but after he put his socks and pants on, he had difficulty with his sweater. As he began to pull the sweater over his head, he had to sit down on the bed because the pain had returned. When I mentioned he should see a doctor, he told me he wanted to wait to see a doctor in Oak Ridge. I replied to him he should not delay medical attention in case it was a serious problem.

The day began with bright blue skies and warm sunshine, yet, by the end of the afternoon, the heavens became gray and dark. My nap was over, and Marie wanted to go the hospital. I said I would after she ate as I was not hungry at all. We decided where we would go, and I commenced driving when the rains came. Rainstorms produce various showers, but this storm seemed to open the heavens, and tremendous downpour was occurring.

We came to an understanding that I would get something to eat at a takeout deli so that I could eat while he was getting medical attention at a nearby hospital emergency room. When we arrived at a deli, it was busy, and I did not want to wait and waste time for Val getting to an emergency room. I returned to the car empty-handed, and Val insisted that he would find a place for me to get something to eat. When he began to pull out of the parking lot, instead of him making a left turn heading back toward town, he made a right turn, heading away from town. I thought, *What in the world is he doing? There is nothing out this way*, but I did not say a word.

After a few minutes, as I looked at him, I asked if he would like me to drive. I thought he looked terrible. He said, "Yes, you'd better," and he stopped the car, got out, walked around the car, and had me scoot over to the driver's seat. I found a spot to turn around so we would be heading back toward town when Val said to me, "Marie, I love you. You better get help and get it quick because I do not think I am going to make it."

I felt a severe sharp pain in the center of my chest. I can only explain the feeling as that of being stabbed with a knife and the blade remaining there, stuck in my chest, causing intense pain.

I thought, *Oh God, I am so scared! What am I going to do?* The traffic was very heavy, and I did not have any idea what to do next. I did not know my way around, and I was so nervous I was shaking all over. It was difficult to see in the darkness of the night. The rain was pouring as the windshield wipers moved at maximum speed. All I could see in front of me was this flashing light, a force pulling me toward it. I did not know what to do; however, the car just moved toward what I thought was a parking lot of a motel. Val got upset at me and said emphatically, "What are you doing? You're not going to find any help here!" I jumped out of the car with words trailing behind me, "Just trust me, Val, trust me."

I saw a group of people standing in front of a motel room door, and I asked them if I could use a telephone. They did not speak English and motioned for me to go to the office of the motel. I ran into the office and said to the young man at the desk, "My husband is having a heart attack. Could you please call for help?" As I ran from the motel office, I could already hear the sound of sirens.

When I got back to the car, I saw Val with his hand out the window catching rainwater and splashing it on his face. He said he was doing this so he would not lose consciousness. By this time, a large number of people had started to gather around. Then I heard people in the crowd that had congregated ask each other if the man was dead or alive. I also heard the replies such as, "He sure looks gone." It was not easy for me to block out the remarks, and they heightened my fear that Val may not survive. I was wearing a red velour warm-up suit and, by this time, was drenched; my clothes weighed a ton. Someone in the crowd handed me a towel. I dipped the towel in a puddle of water and wiped Val's face with it. It was all I could do to keep my wits about myself with all that was happening.

It seemed like an eternity, but it was only a few minutes for the fire department to arrive first. They started oxygen for Val. He tried to explain to them that he could not breathe. The oxygen settings were set for demand rather than on a continuous flow, which was corrected immediately. The ambulance arrived, and as luck would have it, we were next to the highway, which was the shortest route to the hospital. It was a four-mile drive from where we were parked. We were in the right place at the right time because if we had gone the other way toward town, the ambulance would have been stuck in gridlock traffic and unable to pass through.

By 7:30 p.m., Val was in the intensive care unit at the Jordan Hospital in Plymouth having a massive heart attack. I called our friends Rudy and Diane. Rudy is a coworker of Val's, and Diane is a nurse. Diane was aware of the seriousness of the situation and consoled me in a way that left me with the feeling that Val would be all right. I could not see Val or visit him at that time, so Rudy and Diane took me back to the motel where I had left our car. I got into the car and drove back to our hotel where we were staying. I did not get any sleep that night and went to the hospital at seven a.m. I was informed that I would not be able to see Val until the doctor saw him and evaluated his condition.

Dr. Timmers arrived at 8:30 a.m., and upon examination, he informed me that Val was a very sick man and he could not tell me very much. The doctor did inform me that Val had pericardiaditis. Time was of the essence, and the longer that Val stayed alert, the better his chances were.

As word spread of Val's heart attack and his critical condition, telephone calls started pouring in from all over the country. I was asked if somehow the calls could be curtailed because it was an intensive care unit and the telephone lines should not be tied up. Everyone who called, most of whom I did not know, were offering prayers. This was indeed a great comfort. It gave me faith and the strength I needed at the time.

I was unaware of Val's excellent reputation in the nuclear industry. Many of Val's navy assignments were classified, and much of his civilian work highly technical. He did not bring his work home or discuss it with me. In turn, I never revealed any unimportant difficulties I may have had with the children when Val was not home. Our personal life together was very simple and happy. By avoiding the distraction of daily trials and tribulations, we made the most of the little amount of time we had together.

It was difficult for me to believe this was happening. Val was always energetic, outgoing, and seemed indestructible to me. June 1 was an extremely long day. I remained at the hospital all day pacing the long corridors in silent prayer. At 3:00 a.m. on June 2, the nurses suggested that I should go back to the hotel and get some rest. It was no use for me being there since I could not be with Val in the critical care unit.

When I returned to the hotel room where we were staying, I realized how kind the hotel staff was to a stranger in their town. The hotel staff had taped messages all over my mirror and on the glass-topped dresser. This, I thought, took considerable time. It was a comfort in a way, and I sincerely appreciated the kindness. There were so many messages everywhere; I could hardly believe they were all for me. I rested the best I could for a short while then went to an 8:00 a.m. Mass at a nearby church. I was able to see Val that morning but only for a few minutes. Val said to me, "I am so sick."

It was a matter of time to see how Val would progress. I spent the remainder of the day contacting the people who had left messages. I informed them of Val's condition, of which I still knew very little. It was still very important to me that I return the telephone calls. Around 9:00 p.m., I was called to come to the nurse's station. Looking back, I can see they were trying to prepare me for the worst possible outcome. I did not realize it at the time, but now by reflecting on the events, it becomes apparent.

The nurses were asking me when my son from Tennessee was coming, and they insisted, in a nice way, that he should come. I was so far away in Plymouth, Massachusetts, and I had all I could cope with right there at that moment. It was around midnight when I went to the hotel, and again more messages were waiting for me in the same manner as the previous night. I was so exhausted that I fell down on the bed and went to sleep with my clothes on. I was just worn out, both physically and emotionally.

On Sunday morning after Mass, I went to the hospital and sat in a small waiting area in the intensive care unit. There was a patient sitting in a wheelchair. As I sat there crying, a lady named Diane went to the woman in the wheelchair and gave her Holy Communion. When I realized this person was a lay minister, I looked up at her and told her, "I need someone to pray with me. I could not pray in church this morning." The lay minister knelt down beside me and prayed. This was the start of a special friendship. I thanked her for the comfort and prayers and then went back to see if I could get any information on Val.

I could see the doctor talking to Val through the glass window. As the doctor was talking, I could also see Val appeared to be acknowledging everything that was being said to him. His eyes followed the doctor's movements, and his head nodded up and down in acknowledgement. Val was sitting up and appeared to be flushed in the face; however, I thought he looked better than he had the previous day. When I saw Dr. Timmers beginning to leave the room, I proceeded to go in to see Val. Dr. Timmers touched my shoulder and motioned me to the side quickly, out and away from Val's sight through the glass window.

He asked when my son was coming, and I told him that I had no plans for him to come at that particular time. The doctor then suggested he should come, and I replied, "All right, I'll arrange for him to come tomorrow." With that, Dr. Timmers took me by the shoulders, looked me square in the face, and said, "Lady, you haven't heard a darn thing

I've said. I am trying to tell you your husband is in serious danger of dying at any moment. He has an aneurysm in his heart." The doctor proceeded to inform me that anyone who had anything to say to Val should come to the hospital as quickly as possible to see him. He said all this with a sense of urgency that completely caught me by surprise.

Just seconds before I had been thinking that Val looked a little better. The doctor then prescribed some medication to calm me down, and the nurses sat me down to take my vital signs to make sure I was all right. Somehow, after the shock, I managed to contact a few close relatives and arrange for our son Val to come from Tennessee. Our youngest son, Jim, had already planned to be there that day. Jim was attending college about an hour and a half away, and he had visited Plymouth periodically.

Val had no idea the danger he was in, and the urgency of the visits went unnoticed to him. Val accepted the explanations offered by his relatives as to a Sunday drive. Somehow they managed to get through the day without Val having any suspicions, and it seemed like a happy occasion rather than a sad one. Val's two sisters were able to get accommodations at the same hotel that I was staying, and our sons stayed with me for the night. Val's other relatives went back home later in the day.

It was a short night as I was back at the hospital at 6:00 a.m. When I saw Val, he was sitting up in the bed with his legs crossed at the ankle, moving back and forth in a rocking motion. He looked up at me and said, "I am so glad you are here. I've been waiting for you, and I thought

I was never going to see you ever again. I am so sick. I wish I could go to sleep."

I went to the attending physician sitting at the nurse's station reviewing patients' charts and said to him, "My husband never complains, and he really would like to have something to help him sleep, so can you please give him something to make him go to sleep?"

The doctor looked at me and asked, "What do you mean *make him go to sleep?*"

I replied, "Val would like to sleep. Can you do anything for him?"

He explained to me that the nurses had just given him some medication a short time ago. Then he instructed the nurse to go ahead and give him half a dose of pain medication. I went back in to see Val, and while he lay there, I stroked his hair and placed a cool damp cloth on his forehead. After about fifteen minutes, he fell asleep. I left his room feeling bewildered and sad to see Val suffering as he was.

The next few hours were very difficult for me to stay in prayer and focus on the Lord. Val's sisters came to the hospital around 11:00 a.m., and I suggested they go in and see Val since they had a plane to catch in the early afternoon. When they emerged from Val's room, they told me he was no longer on oxygen and the doctor was with him. I had made my mind up already that I did not desire to speak with the doctor, and as he came out of Val's room, I tried to avoid him. As he passed by me, he simply said, "Good." To be certain of what I thought I had heard, I asked, "Excuse me?" The doctor explained to me that his enzyme count was beginning to come down, a good sign that a healing process was beginning. Val remained in the hospital for over two weeks. An appointment was scheduled for the next day in Oak Ridge with a heart specialist.

FLYING WITHOUT OXYGEN

I purposely called the airport in advance to let them know Val needed a wheelchair and that we would be bringing a portable oxygen container to take with us on the plane. Val remained in the hospital until it was time to go to the airport. When we arrived at the airport, the personnel did not have any knowledge of the telephone call, and I had to find a wheelchair for Val. I pushed Val through the security check and laid the portable oxygen case on the conveyor belt of the security machine that checks carry-on luggage at the gate. I was immediately informed that I would not be allowed to carry it onto the plane. I was completely exasperated. We were sent to the boarding gate and told that someone would come and talk to us.

A man approached carrying the oxygen case. As he got closer to me, I noticed Val was looking very pale and gray by this time. The whole situation began to take its toll on him, as well as on me. I was frustrated and even more so when the man told us the tank would need to be emptied of the oxygen before we took it on the plane. Imagine sitting at the boarding gate, Val in a wheelchair as ill as he was, and the oxygen hissing out of a portable tank in front of other passengers waiting to board the plane. It was not a pleasant situation. To make matters worse, there were other obstacles put in front of us. Airport personnel insisted that

Val sign a waiver so if they had to leave him in Cincinnati due to health-related complications, they could. They also tried to convince us to postpone our flight at least to the next day, making us think that our connections could not be made and we would miss our flight. I just knew in my mind Val couldn't miss the appointment with the cardiologist the next day. Now all we could do was wait to see what was going to happen. I was certain we were not going to postpone getting home.

To our surprise, we were met in Cincinnati by a man with a wheelchair to be whisked off to our connecting flight to Knoxville. Upon arriving in Knoxville, we had been promised they would have the oxygen tank refilled with oxygen for Val. What they did not tell us was they would call an ambulance to come to the airport to fill the tank with oxygen at our expense!

Our friends Bob and Joan drove us home to Oak Ridge. They were in shock to see how sick Val looked and started to think about where they could stop if they had to for Val. On the way home, Val covered himself up with a blanket and tried to relax in the car, but he simply could not. I conversed with Bob and Joan, but Val could not comprehend or really hear us clearly. It seemed to him how a centurion would struggle with a foe in his final contest for life.

After an hour of eternity to Val, we arrived home, and he was essentially carried into the house. Our bed had been relocated to the downstairs family room for ease and comfort. I gave Val his medications, undressed him, and he was hardly in bed a moment before drifting off to sleep.

Upon awakening late in the morning, Val looked up

and did not know where he was, initially. It was not the hospital or our bedroom. He was disoriented, confused, and he thought he was alone. He called out, "Marie!" and I came immediately. Val was so relieved. I told him all that had transpired from the airport until that moment.

The haze was suddenly realized by Val, and he felt very strange that he could not remember much until his mind was refreshed with information. Never in his life had he been in a situation like this. Even when he had a few too many on a rare occasion, he could always remember most of what transpired. He said, "When your mind fails, one begins to wonder what will be and what's to be in the days to come."

The appointment with Dr. Robert Gentry of Parkway Cardiology was scheduled for 2:00 p.m. Tuesday, June 19. Val's time at home was spent lying on the bed, listening, and not talking too much. He was having a difficult time doing nothing, just lying there.

When it was time to go, Val was dressed, and off we went to Parkway Cardiology. He was concerned, not nervous. A nurse assisted us to the exam room, and Dr. Gentry entered. It certainly made Val feel good to see a jovial doctor that made him feel very comfortable and relaxed. I went over most of the details of Val's situation, and the doctor replied, "This is normal for most men as they live in a world of self-denial." Then Val knew that he was not the only nincompoop in the world. A heart monitor was fitted on him to record the activity of his heart over the next twenty-four-hour period. There were no changes in the medication he was taking at that time, only a few changes after reviewing the monitor. After consulting with the other cardiologists, they would develop a recovery strategy.

Thursday afternoon, Dr. Gentry called me, informing me of Val's condition. He stressed that Val should have very little activity until they assessed how severe the damage was to the heart as a result of the heart attack in Plymouth.

Look at what happened because I did not go to a doctor when I should have after my initial pains. Live and learn and bearer beware; pay attention to the signs and danger of potential heart problems in any pains.

We were expecting our son Jim and fiancé, Valarie, to visit from Connecticut. Val was very anxious for Jim to come to Oak Ridge, as he felt he could always depend on him. Should the worst scenario take place, he wanted to talk to him and inform him about his wishes, and Val also knew I would like him to be with me. As the week passed, Val felt himself slipping backwards, although he did not express it to anyone. He tried to keep a positive attitude so as not to worry anyone. Most likely, however, they could observe his expressions, behaviors, and chose, like him, not to say anything.

Jim and Valarie arrived Thursday the twenty-eighth, and Val felt greatly relieved. Valarie's smiling face showed concern, as did Jim's, even though they were on the bright and cheery side. This gave Val concern, so he went to look in the mirror later. He did not think he looked differently than he did before the heart attack, except for appearing fatigued. Val had never seen anyone who had experienced what he did and, therefore, did not have comparisons. Besides, Val would have said he looked much better.

The next day, June 29, Val awoke to the feeling of having a lot of mucous in his throat, so he went to the bathroom to clear it. He immediately observed the phlegm had spotty, pinkish color which shocked him. Val called me, and I assisted him back to bed, where he lay back down. I telephoned the doctor right away. Dr. Gentry said this was normal in the recovery process and not to worry. He prescribed medication and instructed me to have Val on complete bed rest for a few days and he would see him in his office on Monday. Val's only comment was that he had more bed rest in the past month than he had the entire previous year. This also meant Val would need to use the urine collection bottle, which was not an easy task in a horizontal position.

Saturday passed with no experiences. Sunday morning, July 1, I came to Val with his 7:00 a.m. medication. He was not feeling well and told me he doubted he could swallow it. I wanted to get dressed and attend 8:00 a.m. Mass, but Val asked me to lie beside him and consider attending a later Mass. I had gotten no real rest in over a month. Whenever Val moved, I would move as well and ask him if he was okay. So that I could rest, he rubbed my forehead and told me he was thinking of the day when he could hold me again and dance with me. I soon went into a deep sleep.

Val decided to get up to go to the bathroom. He sat up quietly for a minute and slowly walked approximately fifteen feet to the bathroom. He felt very weak, but he made it to the bathroom. When he sat down, he started to feel strange, his ears began to ring, his vision became very dull, and then he couldn't see at all. He staggered out of the bathroom and fell into an armchair. He called out to me. I was startled as if I was in a daze. I recall thinking, *Where is that coming from?* I felt disoriented until I realized Val was not in the bed. After realizing it was Val calling my name, I immediately went to him, calling the boys to come downstairs.

Val said he felt numbness in parts of his body, and I assisted him to the floor so he could lie down. Val's color had vanished by this time, and Jim raised his legs to help his circulation. I called 911 for an ambulance, and because I did not leave a confirmation telephone number with the dispatch, I had to call them again. Twenty-five minutes later a neighbor directed the ambulance into our driveway. Val could not see, but he could hear my voice and the family carrying on with excitement. I had to tell them to settle down. Even though Val appeared unconscious, I did not want him to hear anyone speaking of his condition.

PARALYSIS

The ambulance ride to the hospital was quick with the hospital being only three miles from our home. Val's eyesight did not improve, so everything appeared gray and dark. He hoped this was just temporary and kept his eyes closed for most of the time. He did open his eyes when the ambulance attendants spoke to him. Val should have been afraid, but he wasn't. He knew the situation was not good but tried to remain calm to not aggravate his heart's condition any further.

I was in the emergency room for a short time and then taken to the critical care unit, where I was put on oxygen and other intravenous medications and monitors. I know I slept on and off during this time. I felt and I knew things were not going well and I might not survive. I prayed to God for many things, especially my loving wife, Marie. I started thinking about my life and how I had very few regrets.

During the long day as time passed, I continued to think of the many happy times in the early days when our love was young. I recalled all the places we had visited together and of simply enjoying life and not thinking ahead of the later years; however, we did save money for our twilight years. The enjoyments we shared were mostly simple and spontaneous.

Marie is a survivor from a meager life as a child. As a young adult, she took care of her cancer-stricken mother. She raised our children with my long work hours, and frequent traveling certainly took more fortitude than most of us have. I never could imagine her with another man. I would not want to think of that, as it would upset me.

Val's day was long, and his mind was busy with the thoughts of how much he wanted everything to go away and for life to be like it used to be. Val had always planned on taking many long trips, but he never did because of his work schedule and travels. He felt as if he'd missed the boat and it was too late. Many of his old-time friends came to mind and those who had already gone to heaven. One of the changes he would have made in life was for us to do what we would like and put his career second in some cases. These thoughts would make him melancholy, and a nurse would come in to check on Val. She frequently asked him if something was wrong and if he was all right. The monitors sent some signal to the nurse's station that alerted them.

Someone sure can alter one's own mind and send himself into a deep depression. My background had taught me self-control, and that discipline brought me through many of the recent crises. In the past, it was often said to me that I always stayed calm managing difficult tasks. I never thought of this at the time; only now as I reflect back on my past I realize it served me well.

Dr. Gentry came into my room in the intensive critical coronary care unit, and from the serious expression he wore on his face, I could feel my heart pound and throb. In no way was I, nor could I have been, ready for what he was to say. "Mr. Bouchard, I want to discuss your medical condition with you. This is unpleasant for me, but you told me you expect me to always be up front and candid about your health and treatment.

"Your kidneys and liver are failing to function. You have extensive pulmonary edema, a build-up of fluid in your lungs that will slowly continue to get worse and cause you to struggle and fight to breathe. You are going to die tonight."

I replied, "But Dr. Gentry, how can that be? I don't feel that sick."

He responded, "Just wait an hour or two, and you will be suffering in great agony, and I certainly wouldn't want to be the one to care for you and to witness such suffering. What I would like to suggest is to make passing reasonably comfortable for you. That means, place you on a respirator, sedate you, then immobilize you with a medication that paralyzes you so you won't fight death by drowning. It would be a less difficult experience for you and your family."

In his estimation, death would come in about four to five hours. The doctor then asked me what I thought about what he had just explained to me, and I said I had no thoughts and told him that it meant I do not have much to say, except for him to go ahead and proceed. "Please don't tell my wife what you have told me just now. I just can't bear that Marie know at this time."

Dr. Gentry informed me that my family would visit me before proceeding with the procedure. Two nurses accompanied Dr. Gentry; one male, one female. Upon leaving the room, Dr. Gentry gave the order to prepare the respirator and the injection, which would paralyze me.

How can this be the end? I don't feel that sick. Where did it all go? Suddenly, my life flashed before my eyes.

My father died Friday, December 10, 1937, at the age of thirty-two from a case of streptococcus from an operation to remove a cyst off his spine. I recall my father requesting me to come be at his bedside before going to bed that night. I sat there on his bed; he spoke to me with tears in his eyes, saying to me, "Please help your mother, brother, and sisters. Be the best you can be." He spoke to me about various other things that I cannot recall, but I do remember he gave me a nice long hug before I went to bed. In the morning, Aunt Helen, known to me as Other Ma, meaning other mother, brought me downstairs to tell me that my father passed away during the night.

I was a young boy, nine years old with three younger siblings. My youngest sister, Elaine, eighteen months old; my other sister, Terry, almost five years old; and my brother, George, almost four years old. As I look back now, it did not seem like such a sad time. Being told that my father was in heaven did not seem so bad; although, I did not really know much about death either. It was near Christmas time, and I remember the bitter cold outside on the day of the funeral at the cemetery. I was told later it had been ten degrees below zero in Adams, Massachusetts a small town in the northwest region of the state.

Elaine, George, Terry, and Val

I went to catechism at our Catholic Church on Saturday mornings. My friends came to the house for me, and I had to explain to them I would not be going with them because my father died. I noticed a wreath hanging on our front door at that time, and I assumed it was there for the holidays, but I learned later it was because there was a death in the family. Every day at twelve o'clock, the church bells rang; however, on this day, the bells chimed a different sound so the townspeople were aware of a death in the community.

None of us understood money because we did not have any. We ate well from the garden we planted in our small backyard. We were provided with food from the town's welfare supply. It consisted of whatever was in season: potatoes, squash, pumpkins, and apples in the fall and rations of oatmeal, cornmeal, flour, and fruit. No one ever went hungry. We played and had good times with all the other children in the neighborhood. Games like hide and seek, dodgeball, nipsy, and tag kept us busy. The boys ventured up the mountain called Side Hill to our big cliff. There was an array of rope swings, huts, and the best of all, in the summertime, the mud hole. This swimming hole was a depression in the hill that we dammed up with burlap bags full of sand and dirt. The water inlet came from trickling cold water springs and little runoffs through the fields and woods. What a wonderful life.

We never knew we were all poor because nobody ever told us we were poor. We should have suspected something the minute we walked in the front door of the shoe store. For example, the storeowner, Mr. Goldberg, took one look at us guys, and he immediately directed us to the back room of the store. We got to view and choose from his secondhand specials, which meant two-toned, unmatched, and each foot a slightly different size or shape. As young-sters, we all wore the same high-top canvas Ked sneakers. The soles were so well made, they would last for a hundred years; however, you were lucky if the tops lasted you the summer months because your toes poked through the can-vas material after three or four weeks of constant wear.

Mr. Pritz, the neighborhood barber, would literally shave our heads, even after our begging him, "Just a trim, like the other kids," but it was to no avail. After one minute in his chair, we were essentially hairless for another four months. We probably only saw him two times a year, sum-mer and winter. In between visits to the barber, my uncle cut our hair with hand clippers. He would pull our hair so hard it hurt, and I must have looked like I had the mange. We all looked the same.

Each summer I went to live and work on a farm or

an orchard. One summer, I received ten dollars, and this went home with me to give to my mother for household expenses, no luxuries. Every day we went to the general store for the mail and other incidentals we might need at the farm. One day I received four or five letters. This was a lot of mail, and I was delighted; however, I did not remember it was my birthday. My family had mailed me cards for my fourteenth birthday. It was a nice surprise to be remembered like that since I had not seen any of them for the entire summer.

I started to work regularly when I was only nine years old while I was in the third grade. It was at the local grocery store bagging potatoes for little or nothing. I also set up the pins in the bowling alley for three cents a string. Those were many a long day as a child. The local supermarket, a bigger store than others, hired some boys for twenty-five cents an hour. We stocked shelves and bagged groceries. Workdays were three hours after school and on Saturday for a total of twenty-three hours in a week making five dollars, seventy-five cents a week in wages. Summer hours were forty hours for ten dollars a week.

I was fifteen years old when employed by the town to help rebuild the town's roads during the summer months. When I turned sixteen, I went to work for the Berkshire Fine Spinning for fifty cents an hour. I worked after school from 3 p.m. to 10 p.m. and Saturdays from 7 a.m. to 2 p.m. for a total of forty hours a week while still attending school during the weekday hours. I did this for about two years until I enlisted in the navy. I was just seventeen when I entered the navy.

Thoughts of school came back to me: first grade with Miss Marley, second grade with Miss Goodermote, third grade with Miss Foisy, fourth grade with Miss Urbanik, fifth grade with Miss Lewis, and sixth grade with Miss Boeam. I never knew until later years that women teachers were not permitted to marry. To all of us, school was wonderful, with plays, singing, and learning. I do remember now how dedicated the teachers were, priding themselves in teaching the fundamentals of life to all. Miss Foisy was strict, and I had my hand swatted with a wooden ruler many times.

I thought especially of the Bible as I lay awake reminiscing of my life. Miss Foisy frequently read Psalm 23 out loud to the class. It became a favorite Bible verse for me, and I recite it every day in my daily prayers. I continued to think back to the days when I grew up.

The economic times were bad, as I now know. The neighborhood was essentially all the same in the way of economic status. Everyone shared whatever we had. We wore hand-me-down clothes and shoes.

Other Ma and Aunt Barbara, as we called our loving mother's aunts, lived upstairs in the four tenement house that was built in 1902. I thought back to our comfortable four-room apartment and compared it to my present two-car garage. It's unbelievable to think and know that our garage is bigger, has more electrical outlets, and has more lights than we had in our entire home where I grew up. The walls are insulated, a luxury never thought of during the times back then. The ice used to build up on the windows, and my brother and I would scrape off the ice with our fingernails, and often we'd entertain ourselves by trying to see who could scrape the biggest piece off. A big piece would be the size of a nickel! The sheets were ice cold when we climbed into bed at night. What a thrill! The only heat for the back bedrooms where we slept came from the kitchen at the front of the house. Later, Other Ma provided us with flannel sheets, so we went without the "thrill" of the ice-cold sheets, a welcome change.

Val with Aunt Barbara, Uncle Frank and Other Ma

Val's family and friends were waiting in silence and prayer at the hospital. No word was received all day long about Val's condition. I stayed in prayer with my rosary and prayed for all the souls in purgatory and felt guilty I could not offer prayers for my husband. At about 8:30 p.m., I went home to get some rest and was just getting out of my car when young Val came back home and told me that I was needed back at the hospital right away. Dr. Gentry met me as soon as I arrived at the hospital and said he wanted to put Val on a respirator. I asked Dr. Gentry if Val was cognitive, and he replied, "Yes, he is." I then told Dr. Gentry that since he already had Val's answer, then he really did not need to have my answer and Val's answer and decision on the matter should be respected.

Dr. Gentry said, "I want you to know that I told Mr. Bouchard he is probably going to die tonight and being put on a respirator will make it easier."

I interrupted him. "Oh, Dr. Gentry, tell me you didn't say that to him."

"Yes, I did. He has a right to know."

"Perhaps you're right."

Dr. Gentry said that he did not want to be the person to care for Val if he chose not to have a respirator because, in that instance, it would be a horrible and agonizing way to die. Dr. Gentry then said he would take the family in to say what could be a final farewell, and these words would probably be the last ones the family could say to Val and that Val could say to the family. My thoughts were, *Lord, you have given me a heavy task this time. I ask you to hold me up, make me strong, and not let me cry, as you know my tears are the only things that Val could never stand to see. I thank you for the twenty-seven beautiful years. Please give me the words I need to say in just a few minutes.*

The room where Val lay was very brightly lit around his

head and darker at his feet. Val tried to speak at the same time I was telling him, "I believe in miracles, Val."

Val said to me, "I know you do, Marie, but it doesn't seem likely this time."

"You don't know that; only God knows." I turned to Dr. Gentry and said, "I am a Christian girl, and I believe in miracles."

Dr. Gentry said, "I had a miracle walk out of this room once before. I will lead this family in prayer."

After the prayer, I said to Val, "The doctor has work to do. Are you ready?"

Val replied to me, "No, but what choice do I have?"

I said, "Precious time is being wasted, and we really should let the doctor get started. I will see you soon." I looked at him and so badly wanted to kiss him one more time on the lips, but I could not bring myself to remove his oxygen mask for that to even be a possibility. So I instead lifted his hand and kissed it so as not to take his air from him. Then the family left the room in a hurry so the doctor could make Val comfortable. I told Dr. Gentry I was going to call a priest and requested Val be put to sleep before the sacrament of Extreme Unction was administered by the priest. Dr. Gentry assured me that he would do as I requested.

I felt as though I was going to collapse and cried bitterly after I left the intensive care unit. I was leaving my husband with both of us knowing the severity of the situation and with neither of us letting the other one know how we were really feeling about what we both knew could be the inevitable. This left me with a deep and painful sadness.

I made the necessary but painful telephone calls to family members and told them to prepare to come to Tennessee for a funeral—Val's funeral.

I placed a call to our friend Dick in Vermont and told him, "I have been told that Val is going to die tonight. I am going to ask you to do something for me that is beyond all your principles and beliefs. If you say yes, it would make me very happy, and if you say no, I will respect that too."

"What do you want?" Dick asked.

"I would like you to pray for Val and ask God to make a miracle happen for him."

"Yes, I will pray for him and for you too."

I thanked him and said, "I will keep you informed the best I can under the circumstances."

That evening I had the boys unplug the telephone downstairs so if the telephone rang I would not have to answer it. The boys could answer the telephone in the upstairs bedroom. Although we had a bed set up downstairs in the family room, I slept on the couch.

I wanted to talk and say many things to prolong the inevitable. Marie told me Dr. Gentry wanted to give me some medicine to relax me and we should not delay the doctor. How much I longed to hold her in my arms and tell her, "Thanks for being my wife," but the boys led her out of the room. How empty I felt. *My world is shattered and gone*, I thought. I continued thinking and said a silent prayer, begging, *God, please watch over her.* I became very distraught. The nurses came to me and asked me to relax. They spoke of hope and prayers. This respirator was unfamiliar and very different to the kind of respirators I used to work within the nuclear industry. This respirator was breathing for me and lessened my struggle to breathe. The realization that this was *life support* set in and made me understand how delicately I was clinging to life.

The paralyzing injection gave me a strange feeling. I could not move at all, not a toe or a finger slightly. I drifted in and out of sleep constantly. I could not see anything, but I could hear when someone entered the room and could hear some voices speaking in low tones. Due to paralysis, my eyes remained open, and I could not blink. The remedy to prevent my eyes from drying out was to place moist pads over them.

I had no sense of time, but it seemed like an eternity. Suddenly, I started to gurgle slightly, and soon it became louder. The nurses came in, removed the respirator, and inserted a vacuum tube into my nose. What happened next was horrible, and I do not wish it upon anyone in his or her life.

It alarmed me to discover that my hands and body were secured to the bed. I could not move, leaving me to feel as though I was at their mercy. I was indeed. A tube was inserted in my nose and passed down into my lung to pump fluid out, and, in doing so, a lung collapsed. This felt like having the wind knocked right out of me. It was not a pleasant experience. I hurt badly and was scared, thus I struggled for breath, which eventually came to me. After only a brief rest, the process began again. This time fluid was removed from the other lung. This procedure was done numerous times throughout the next days.

My kidneys failed to function properly, and the fluid was building up rapidly in both lungs. It was difficult for the nurses to keep up with the pumping process. Each time I started to gurgle, I panicked because I knew what was going to happen. This gurgling noise had been termed by people I knew as the "death rattle." I tried to breathe slower, but I could not control the respirator. It breathed for me at a certain pace, a pace set by a machine and not a pace set by me. I sometimes thought it would be easier to die.

I knew how much time had passed by my sons' visits to me. My son Jim would talk to me and say either, "The weather is nice today," or, "The weather was hot today." I was able to make the distinction between morning or after-noon and evening by these simple sentences. I knew my other son, Val, was present because the boys would con-verse, yet he did not speak directly to me.

Jim recited poetry to me on occasions. This surprised me, and I wondered how and when Jim became interested in that particular poem unbeknownst to me. Later, I dis-covered the Irish Blessing was on the wall in the ICCU room. Jim often read that particular poem to me:

> May the road rise to meet you.
> May the wind be always at your back.
> May the sun shine warm upon your face.
> May the rain fall soft upon your fields.
> And until we meet again
> May God hold you in the palm of his hand.
> Amen

After some time, my neck began to hurt because of the

position I was lying in. It began to ache constantly, and I tried to signal my distress to someone, but to no avail. I thought I could move my finger enough for someone to notice and realized that it was only my thoughts moving my finger and not the finger itself. It was not until I gurgled that I got some relief to my neck since they had to move my head to remove the respirator.

It seemed like I slept longer, and I wondered to myself, *How much longer is this going to go on?* The lung pumping, the pain, and the waiting were making me think of peace and rest. I was ready to see my folks. It had been over fifty years since my father went away.

Some time later, I became aware that Jim was in the room because he was talking as usual. Then I noticed his voice seemed to fade away. It became difficult to hear his voice. I remember straining to listen and figured he must be farther away, perhaps in the hallway. Then I heard nothing.

The next thing I knew, I was walking down a gradual slope on a dirt path looking out onto a large field with tall grass. A fog prevented me from seeing very far; however, I could see sunlight on top of the fog. I kept walking along the dirt path. The fog diminished, and I entered a wooded area. It was clear now, and I could see all around me. Every short distance, the path would direct me to the left or the right.

At one point, I heard faint voices then moaning and then music. The music sounded like a piccolo or a flute, and then a harp was playing. *Very nice*, I thought to myself. I did not know how much further this would go. It was quiet all around me. Suddenly, I found myself in a beautiful clearing with more woods all around. As I proceeded to walk slowly, I came upon some stone steps in front of me.

A man was there. I was surprised. He appeared to stand on or about the third step. I knew it was a man because he had a beard. He said to me, "Welcome to our rest. Do not move; kneel until I say arise." Next, many people came. As I knelt with head bowed, I felt a strong desire to look upwards to see faces of the people, but I could not look up. I could not move my head at all. I assumed they were wearing robes because of what I could see. There were many gathering. I tried to look sideways. Since I could only move my eyes, my vision was limited to peripheral vision. From what I could see, there were brown, tan, and cream colored robes. No shoes, sandals, or footwear of any kind worn by anyone, and I thought to myself, *What is happening or going on?* It puzzled me to see all the feet were so clean, despite all the walking on dirt. No one spoke. It was peaceful, so I closed my eyes and thought, *What sort of dream could this be?* It amazed me when I opened my eyes to see a white robe standing in front of me. I had not heard any noise during my quiet time to indicate that someone was there. I tried to look up again, now for the third time, but I could not move my head. I wondered, *Could this be a point of judgment or heaven?*

I heard a voice say, "Francis, we have been watching you." Francis is my middle name. My father's name was Val, and my family often referred to me as Francis. I was asked, "What do you desire?"

I replied, "I am lost, and I am looking for my folks to see them all again." Some time passed, and it was all silent.

I then became aware of the flute and the harp music playing quietly.

A voice, seeming very close but not in front of me, said, "Go and return home. It is not your time." Everyone disappeared.

I discovered that I was back in my bed at the hospital. The respirator was still functioning properly. I thought to myself, *What a strange dream; it did not seem like a dream.* It was as if I was actually at the places that I dreamt. Was it a dream? I could not help myself from feeling I went to the other side and was sent back. Not being aware of the time of day, the date, or having any idea of how long I had been in the hospital made it seem as though it was a month. In reality, it was only a few days.

I thought to myself, *What a lousy way to survive.* I lost my desire to pray as often as I had been, so I allowed myself to sleep more.

On Monday, July 2, when the boys came downstairs, they said to me, "Dad must still be with us because we didn't get a call from the hospital during the night." We decided to stop by the hospital before going to 8:00 a.m. Mass.

Dr. McLaughlin greeted us when we arrived and said, "Mrs. Bouchard, I wish I could give you some good news, but the situation is grave. Your husband's kidneys and liver are failing, and toxic poisoning has begun to set in. It's just a matter of time, most likely today."

The boys inquired of the doctor whether or not he could perform surgery, dialysis, or something for their father. The doctor told them their father was too weak to survive surgery and to start dialysis would only be a temporary effort. I said to the boys, "Please, it is hard enough for the doctor to have to tell us this sad news, and we shouldn't be asking for something that is beyond his control. All we can do now for your father is pray."

I then asked Dr. McLaughlin what he would suggest for me to do at this time. He suggested we go home and wait for the call. I felt crushed and numb because the only place I wanted to be was there with Val. On that spot, I silently made a covenant with God. He was sending me away from the only place I wanted to be, and I would go home and learn patience like I never knew before, and I would not ask any questions of the doctors or the nurses. I would not go back to the hospital unless God himself sent for me.

The boys knew that I wanted to go to the navy recruiter's office, and Jim offered to go with me. Young Val went home with the rest of the family. I knew that if I went home to read my survivor's benefits plan, it would just be words that wouldn't sink in, that I'd only see words on a piece of paper. Val was retired from the military and would have a military funeral, so I decided to go directly to the recruiter's office and get whatever information I could. The recruiter gave me the name of a gentleman who could assist me and who would handle the funeral arrangements. The recruiter also told me the gentleman would be looking out for my best interests at a time like this.

As Jim and I were leaving the recruiter's office, Val showed up, and I tried to send both of them home. I told the boys I intended to get a set of black rosary beads and I wanted them blessed at the church. I also said I had another errand I wanted to run. Val asked, "Is your errand to go to a funeral parlor?"

"Why yes!"

"I've already called one, and I will take you there."

He took me to a mortuary a short distance away. I informed a gentleman there about what was happening and asked him if he would be willing to handle the arrangements, and I gave him the name of the man the recruiter gave to me. He picked up a death certificate and told us we should fill it out. I was horrified. I said that my husband was still with us. He explained that it would be easier for me since it would give him the authority to claim Val's body if the death certificate was already filled out. Otherwise, I would have to go to the hospital before he did. It then made sense to me that if Val died, I really did not need to go to the hospital because people waiting in the intensive care area did not really need to see me with my tears. I chose to fill out the death certificate with only the minimal amount of information he needed and decided the rest could be done later.

We went straight home from the mortuary without stopping to get the rosary beads. The boys came downstairs with a set of rosary beads in hand, and one said, "Here are Dad's rosary beads; use these." They had found them in a military memorabilia box, and I had forgotten all about them. They were given to Val by his uncle, who obtained them during the invasion of Italy. They were handmade and had been blessed by the pope. After time, the twine had deteriorated a little, and the rosary required some mending. Young Val was able to reattach the first bead and the crucifix together. I then took the rosary beads and kept it clutched in my hand as I prayed the rest of the day.

A neighbor had taken Val's military uniform to the cleaners to be dry cleaned and returned it to me that same day. This gave us time to attach his ribbons to his uniform.

At 11:20 a.m., I received a telephone call from a beautiful Christian man named Tom. He asked me over the telephone if I would accept Jesus as Lord and personal Savior all the days of my life and make him second to none. I said without hesitation I would, and I knew that everything in my life needed to be second to my Lord and I had to serve my Lord above all things. Until then, I had not realized my priorities were wrong, that I had put my family first. Tom also encouraged me that miracles do happen and I should keep the faith.

At noon, Val's good friend, Bob, came to the house to see me, and I talked to him in the driveway. I had confided in him that since Val traveled so extensively, we had not had our wills signed in the presence of an attorney. He asked me what I was going to do. I said, as I looked up at the sky, that if God wanted me to live in a tent without a dime, so be it.

I asked him if he would take me to the church to see the priest. I talked to the priest about the church service and my music preferences. I was concerned about the recessional song, whether or not it would be appropriate. I only wanted the instrumental part of "Laura's Theme" from *Doctor Zhivago* played without the words being sung. The priest said it could be done but it was very heavy in his opinion. He also gave me permission to deliver the eulogy as I had requested. This seemed very brave to me, since I had not yet mustered up the courage to do a Sunday liturgy reading in church, but for this, I felt confident.

Tom called me frequently that day, and in one of the conversations, he asked me what I thought about Satan. I told him that not only had I never really given him much thought one way or another, but I didn't have time now to give Satan any consideration at all. He told me I should beware of Satan, and I decided he might be right and should not shut out the idea.

As I started to become aware of what Tom told me, I could begin to see different things that happened that could get in the way of my believing a miracle could indeed occur. I did not want to lose sight of the idea of a miracle and could see how things were trying to knock me down and make me accept the true reality of the situation. I, on the other hand, felt I was accepting reality. Monday was a tough day to get through, but with a lot of prayer, hope, determination, and grace, the day finally ended. Praise be to Jesus.

Every day I went to Mass at St. Mary's Church with the family. The hospital Val was staying in was located in between the church and our home. That meant twice a day I had to pass in front of the hospital. It was a test of my willpower and my trust in God for me not to stop at the hospital on any occasion going to or from the church to ask questions of the doctors and the nurses. I felt good that Val was in God's hands at the hospital.

On Tuesday, July 3, I gathered everyone together at home. The day was beautiful and sunny, so I told everyone there would be no moping around and we would get the house and the grounds ready for whatever we had to face. Things were done with seemingly little effort and a lot of cooperation.

The boys left to go to the hospital that afternoon around four thirty, and I gave young Val his father's rosary beads, telling him they might give him strength. I was talking on the telephone with a friend from Massachusetts at around seven thirty when the boys came home. I could tell they had been crying, and I asked them, "Is your father gone?" They replied that they came home to be with me when I got the call.

"What do you mean?" I asked.

Jim said, "The blood pressure machine indicator dropped dramatically, and the respirator seemed to be the only thing moving dad's chest up and down. He seemed lifeless."

I then asked them, "So, it isn't confirmed yet?"

Jim said, "No, we wanted to be with you when you got the call. Mom, it was beautiful. Val and I went to church, and I never saw my brother on his knees for so long, ever."

Jim had emptied his dad's bottle of nitroglycerin and filled it with holy water and sprinkled it all over his father. Val had soaked the twine rosary in holy water and put it around his father's neck. Jim had put his St. Christopher medal around his father's neck; then they both gave him up to the Lord.

Jim said that besides the other problems his dad was experiencing, his temperature was 107 degrees. With it being so elevated, even if he did recover, he would most likely have brain stem damage, causing him to become a vegetable. He knew his father would never want to live like that.

I said, "Since it is not confirmed, I want you two boys to get away from me. Satan is trying to use you to make me lose faith and not believe that God can do all things. God has not given me the answer yet, and until he does, I will believe he can do all things because the Bible is his true inspired Word. The good book tells us that Jesus raised the dead and broke fevers, and I believe that to be true. I believe in what I have never seen."

Jim said, "Mom, you are not facing reality. Val and I gave Dad up to the Lord tonight, and it was beautiful. Dad would not want to be a vegetable and just sit in a chair or lay in a bed the rest of his life. Now he will have a chance to meet your mother and father for the first time and be with his mother and father, Auntie Barbara and Other Ma, Uncle Max, and he will be so happy."

I thought what a beautiful talk the boys must have had together and how I wished I could have been with them. I said, "I am facing reality, and I want you to leave me be." I walked out into the backyard and knelt down under a flowering plum tree and cried bitter tears. I prayed, *God, I believe with all my heart that you can do all things; let your will be done, and do what's best for us all. My whole body is breaking into a million pieces, and the pain seems more than I can endure. I know whatever you decide will be a miracle, for if you leave Val with us, it will be a miracle for a lot of people to see, and if you take him with you into your arms, it will be a miracle for Val. What greater reward can anyone have than to come home to you? I also know I have no right to ask you for something that belongs to you and will try to conduct myself in a manner you will be proud of and will not kick up my heels over your decisions, so let your will be done.*

At that moment, it was as though someone placed a hand on my shoulder. It felt warm, and I stood up with a peace unlike any I had ever known or felt before. It was so beautiful, and I was forever changed. I no longer had any fear of what was going to happen or about what the outcome would be.

Jim and Val had gone back into the house, and when I went in, Jim was on the telephone. I could hear him say, "I want confirmation about my dad, and I want it now." He restated what he had tried to tell me earlier about the machine's readings when he and his brother left the hospital to come home to me. All of a sudden, Jim cried out, "I don't believe it!" He was laughing and crying at the same time.

I said to Jim, "Tell me quick. I will believe it. Jim, what is it?"

"Well, the nurse said that Dad has not changed one way or the other since this afternoon. He's in limbo, no better, no worse. The blood pressure machine had malfunctioned, so they had to get another one to replace it."

There were a lot of telephone calls coming in the house that evening, and I don't know how I knew, but I knew everything would be okay. I had no negative feelings with each ring of the telephone, and I got myself ready for bed. For the first time, I wanted to sleep in our bed downstairs in the family room. I now felt so secure and trusting that I put the telephone beside the bed and laid my head on my husband's pillow. I went to sleep so peacefully that night for the first time since Val's heart attack in May. I did not wake up until 5:00 a.m. I got up, went to the bathroom, looked at the clock, and figured that I still had another hour that I could sleep. I did not get up until it was time to get ready for church. I was rested and felt good. It was a very peaceful night.

We all went to church together that particular morning of July 4 but not because it was a holiday. We simply wanted to go and be together. The priest spoke about miracles in his homily to my utter amazement. The story the priest talked about was about the story of Lazarus. "This sickness will end not in death, but in God's glory and through it the Son of God will be glorified" (John 11:4).

I was soon brought to tears with excitement and overwhelming joy as I listened to the priest deliver his homily. The boys tried to get me to settle down, but I could not contain the excitement I felt. As I left church, I approached Father Gahagan and said to him with exhilaration, "Father, we are witnessing a miracle." His response to me was, "Walk with the Lord; don't run ahead of him."

My joy suddenly vanished, and I was reigned in to a quiet mood. When I traveled home, I wanted desperately to stop at the hospital to see Val. This was the first time for me that the temptation to stop was overpowering, but I denied the enticement and continued home.

A friend and constituent of Val's, Gene, brought a tape recorder for me to tape the eulogy. After church at 8:45 a.m., I picked up the tape recorder off the kitchen table.

I sat outside on the rear deck of our home to record what I felt was Val's contributions to his family, friends, and to society. Gene came by the house at eleven to see how we were getting along, and I told him then that I had made the tape. He took it along with him to have his secretary transcribe the recorded tape.

I heard someone enter the room without speaking a word, so I thought it must be a nurse. I had been lying on my back for the entire time I was in the hospital. The person in the room took hold of my right hand, and I knew instantly it was my brother, George.

I do not recall us ever holding hands, but we must have done so early in life. I am sure my mother told us more than once, while making ready to cross a street, to hold hands after looking both ways. We would always greet each other with a hug upon seeing one another on infrequent visits. I wanted so much to squeeze his hand back; however, I still could not move. The paralyzing medicine I was given still had its effect on me.

I got very emotional, which set off some of the monitors' alarms and, thereby, alerted the nurses at their station, and people came running into my room. They could not believe such a response from me given my desperate condition. I was not given any more of the paralyzing medication after the last dose slowly wore off.

My family from up north was granted permission to visit me at this time. I was glad they were there, but I wanted my Marie to come be with me. I was writing her name in the air, even dotting the letter i, and my sister Terry finally discerned that I wanted Marie. My family knew then that I was able to communicate with limitations, as I was still blind with wet patches over my eyes. A nurse then provided me with a clipboard and paper on which to write. I wrote the best I could, but sometimes I went beyond the edges of the paper on the clipboard. These are some words I wrote on the paper. I keep the piece of paper in a scrapbook. This documents the entire ordeal:

Ice

I cannot talk

I am I so sick

What are you going to give me?

Jim, U Tenn, go home

I am going to sleeeeeep. [When writing "sleep," I did in fact drift off to sleep.]

At 11:45 a.m., our son Val came to me and said that his father wanted me to come to the hospital. I asked, "How do you know that? I can't understand how he is sending for me, Val, since he can't talk; he's on a respirator."

"Uncle George's wife called. They just arrived at the hospital and are in with Dad now."

"I told God on Monday, I would not go back to the hospital unless he sent for me. However, I will go with you, but you must go in first and let me know if the Lord sent for me or if your dad's family wanted me to come because I haven't been there since Monday."

Val asked me, "How am I going to do that? How will I let you know the Lord has sent for you?"

I answered him, "I haven't the foggiest idea."

Arriving at the hospital, Val went in to see his father, and soon I heard him coming back down the hall, saying, "Praise Jesus, Alleluia!"

I said, "Yes, praise Jesus and Alleluia for what?"

Val then replied, "My father's blue eyes are open again!"

With those words, I went in to see my husband. On the way in, young Val said, "My brother got his prayers answered, and he will get to see our father's blue eyes again." I just knew this was a sign that the Lord did intend for me to be there now. Val's sister said he had been writing my name with his finger in the air, and he even dotted the letter *i*. This information came to me later that evening, and it gave silent affirmation of my seeing Val that day. I was convinced that it was of God. Terry said it took them a little while to determine what it was he was trying to convey to them, but they realized he dotted the *i* every time.

Val's brother, George, had decided to stop by the hospital upon arriving in town to see if the hospital had any information about the arrangements. Instead, they found out their brother was still alive, and there was a lot of rejoicing in the parking lot. George went back in the hospital to see if they could see their brother. The nurse told him, "Yes, you can see him, but he won't know you're here." When George went into the room to see his brother, he silently touched Val's hand, and Val did not know how he knew, but he knew it was his brother. Val got so emotional the alarms on the medical equipment started to sound, bringing the nurses in on a run. They could not believe Val's response. All the family was permitted to visit at this time.

I told Val about all the nice food I had prepared for his

family. I knew this would give Val great satisfaction knowing they would be enjoying some favorite foods that his family used to prepare. It would also comfort Val to know that I was not simply sitting at home crying all day long.

A fascinating thing occurred that day. Gene's secretary, Susan, dropped by the house and gave me the typed copy of my earlier recording. As I began to read the paper she handed me, I could not believe my eyes. I thought I had recorded in the past tense about what I felt he was as a father, friend, and a humanitarian. This mystified me, but I continued to read the paper, and what I was reading presented itself as a letter to Val rather than about him. The letter reads, in part, as follows:

> My Dearest Darling Val,
>
> I'm sitting on our back porch. I have asked God for a miracle for you. I have asked God to spare you for us and that, if he would grant us that wish and make a miracle happen because it is going to take a miracle to bring you back to us, that you would be a wonderful instrument in being a crusader for God and you would come to know God truly through this experience. So many people all over the country have been praying for you. The calls that come in, and the people say how they love you, how they have been up all night praying for you, saying the rosary—it's unbelievable. I have a calm about myself today because I went to church. The priest said, "They that do not see, but believe . . ." And I do believe in miracles. I do believe in God's will, and it's in his hands, my darling.

This made me especially anxious to see and talk to Val about the letter from the recording. After dinner, I returned to the hospital for a private visit with Val before the rest of the family arrived. I shared part of the letter with him, and I asked him if he believed a miracle was happening. He nodded, so I knew we were in union about the miracle.

I was surprised at how well he communicated by writing, and I wiped his face with a cool damp cloth and put some lip balm on his dry, cracked lips. I also was able to put a few very small pieces of ice in the side of his mouth. The slightest amount of liquid Val consumed could have dire consequences given his condition. When Val continued to nod his head up and down to indicate yes, I began to wonder that with his dangerously elevated temperature if his mind was okay or not. I decided to ask him a different question. "When they sedate you, are you more comfortable?" He shook his head no so hard he nearly shook himself right out of bed. That response with the look of frustration on his face convinced me that he was of sound mind. After visiting hours were over, we all went home to get some rest. Val's family drove nineteen hours nonstop to get to Oak Ridge and were completely exhausted. We were all very tired and were content to sleep soon after going home.

> July 4, 1984
> Dear Marie:
> It was good of you to call me this evening. I feel that the crisis has now been passed and that it is now a matter of time and good care.
> My "prayers" were constructed on the trust

that the doctors and nurses would have the skill and knowledge to help make the miracle possible.

Your faith is beautiful to behold, and if ever it is justified it is now. I feel we all can rest a little easier now and that faith will surely carry Val all the way now.

I will be "praying" for him and that you too will continue strong and that your faith will carry you through.

All my love,
Dick

I awoke the morning of July 5, and I quietly got myself ready for church. I made a pot of coffee, set some rolls and jams out with a note for everyone to help themselves. After church, I stopped by the office where Val worked to give them an update on his condition. I was handed a picture of Val, taken on May 17, and I asked them if they were still going to do the article for the corporate publication. It touched me when they indicated they were intending to print the article. I could never thank those people enough for the love and support I received from them during the crisis.

Everyone was having breakfast when I returned home, and I joined them. I was given a pleasant surprise: George was going to cook dinner for us so I would have a rest. After breakfast, I pampered myself with a haircut, doing my nails, and having quiet time by myself. I went for the afternoon visit alone, and I told Val that I would not be back in the evening, unless his condition changed. I wanted to allow his family the opportunity to visit with him during those visiting hours. Val nodded in agreement.

George and the two boys visited Val at 5:00 p.m. When they returned home, George told me that Val wanted encouragement that he was doing better.

I asked, "How do you know, George, that Val wants to know this?"

George replied, "We are all telling him that he is doing better, but I think he really wants to hear it from the doctor."

I subsequently found out this was not what Val had wanted; rather, he wanted the doctor to have to explain what was happening only one time to everyone together and not have to repeat himself. Val was simply trying to be considerate of the doctor's precious time.

I said to George, "I will take care of this." I telephoned Dr. Gentry's answering service only to discover he had left for a vacation the Monday following the Sunday evening he had remained with Val. He was with Val through the night. This did not catch me by surprise or cause me any concern because Dr. Gentry did not owe me any explanation of his vacation plans. Keep in mind, I was not asking any questions of the doctors or nurses. Val had superb care from all the physicians in the cardiology group.

The answering service provided me with Dr. Barry's home telephone number since he was the physician on call that evening. I placed a call to his home, and his wife informed me that he was out for a jog and she asked me if I would like her to page him for me. I said no, but when he returned, I asked if I could have a few minutes of his time and left my telephone number with her. Suddenly,

I got scared and remembered my covenant I had made with God about not talking to any doctors or nurses about Val. I wanted Val to be reassured that night by the doctor about his condition so he could possibly sleep better. I told George that when the telephone rang, he would have to answer it and speak to Dr. Barry himself. When Dr. Barry called, I could tell by the conversation that Dr. Barry would not be going to the hospital that night. My thoughts were, *Please go and give Val some words of encouragement.*

THE PHONE CALL

The rest of the family went to visit Val at the hospital while I stayed home in prayer. I prayed that somehow in some way Val would get some kind of encouragement that night. The boys came home first, and young Val said, "Uncle George has something to tell you when he gets home. Don't worry, it's not bad; it's good."

When George arrived he said, "You're not going to believe what happened."

I said, "Oh, yes I will. What is it?"

"We all left Val's room when my wife forgot something and we had to go back into his room to retrieve it. As we said good night to Val, a nurse walked in with a cordless phone and put it up to Val's ear. Since Val could not talk, all he could do was listen and nod his head. When he handed the telephone back to the nurse, he was motioning it to me. It was Dr. Gentry calling from his parents' home in Virginia. He said, 'I don't know exactly what has been going on, but your brother should not have been here three days ago. I told him I will see him Monday morning.'"

With this wonderful good news, I just knew we had a miracle happening.

On Thursday evening, July 5, Dr. Gentry telephoned the nurse's station from his folks' house in Virginia while he was on vacation. The nurse brought the telephone in to me and held the receiver up to my ear so I could hear what he wanted to tell me. Doctors Fred Barry and Victor McLaughlin had kept Dr. Gentry informed of my condition and progress. He gave me hope and said I had passed a major crisis. He did not say what would come next, and I could not ask him. He told me he would see me on Monday the ninth.

My time was only hanging on by the minute, and Monday seemed like light years away. I pointed to my brother, and he took the telephone, and they spoke for a period. Not knowing what was going on, I tried to watch George's face to see any expression that exhibited some kind of emotion one way or another as he conversed with Dr. Gentry. It frustrated me not to notice any change in George's expression. George conveyed his conversation with Dr. Gentry and that his advice was for us all to be patient and I was in good care with Parkway Cardiology. He further explained to George that he had planned to stabilize me so I could be treated at a facility equipped to care for my condition. I, at least, knew this much: with the extensive damage to my heart, there was only a slim chance I could survive any kind of open heart surgery. My total weight loss between May 31 and July 5 was thirty-four pounds. This was a significant amount, and George explained that my body could not survive the trauma of surgery.

That night at eight thirty, I received a telephone call from our dear friend Tom. Tom asked if it would be okay if his prayer partner, Paul, could call me. I said, "I would welcome it." Paul telephoned right away, and I told him I believed a miracle was happening. He said to me, "By faith we are healed." He also said he had personally witnessed some of the miracles we read about in the Bible.

Paul traveled all over the world taking nothing with him, just like the apostle Paul, preaching the Word of God. He gave up a good job to study the Old and New Testament. One project was especially dear to him: the Shroud of Turin. We spoke on the telephone for over an hour, and he never once mentioned the length of the long-distance call he had made to me, a total stranger. What he said left me with incredible power to put behind my hope and faith and with the positive attitude that our miracle would continue and the reassurance that Val would be well.

As good as I was feeling, the telephone rang after Paul's phone call, and this time it was Val's friend, Bob. That put me down in the dumps, as well intentioned as he was. He was trying to look out for my welfare and for my best interests. He asked me to consider having Val sign our wills now that he was able to write. I indicated to Bob I could not do that with him being so sick. I just could not perform an act like that, but I understood that he was only trying to protect me.

On Friday July 6, I received a call from the hospital. With no explanation as to why, they asked me to come. I had butterflies in my stomach, and my legs felt weak and shaky as I hurried to the intensive care unit.

Upon entering, the nurse told me Val was asking for me and it would be okay for me to go in and visit him. I walked into Val's room, and tears of joy filled my eyes. I noticed that the respirator had been removed, and he mouthed the words *I love you*. I could not hear the words since his voice was so weak. No sound came out. I thought, *Oh Lord, what a beautiful gift you have allowed me to have.* I am short, so I placed a stool beside the bed, climbed up, kissed him on the lips, and held him again. Words can never describe my emotions at that moment.

Val motioned me to put my ear up to his mouth, and he asked me when I come back for the next visit to bring him an orange Popsicle. I told him, "You can't have any Popsicles." He nodded yes, so I asked the nurse to be sure if he could. She said, "Yes, little pieces." When I returned for the next visit, I had forgotten about the Popsicle. He said to me, "My Popsicle." I felt terrible that I had forgotten. After scurrying around town looking for an orange Popsicle, all I could find were banana-flavored Popsicles, and this was just what he told me he did not want since that was the only flavor he had been getting at the hospital. He was tired of banana and wanted orange. My son Val was able to find a cherry-flavored Popsicle for his father after his request for any flavor other than banana.

On Friday afternoon, the sixth, the respirator was removed, and after close observations, it was determined that I could finally breathe on my own without the aid of a machine. It was not a pleasant experience—similar to the process of the lung suctioning. It caused great discomfort, and I gagged severely. My lungs and throat were vacuum pumped again, and it was just as horrible as the first time. I hoped then and still hope to never experience that again.

I still could not see very well, and my throat was extremely sore. I could only speak with a quiet whisper. My lips were dry and cracked. They applied a lubricant to my lips to promote healing. I was given only a sparse amount of liquid in my daily diet, so I was only provided with small amounts of ice chips to soothe my mouth and throat.

It gave me a mental boost that my sisters, brother, and his wife were with me. The first couple days they spoke about many stories from when we were growing up. They laughed, and hearing their laughter lifted my spirits. It was good for all of us to share those moments. Since the work I did involved frequent travel and there was physical distance between our homes, we visited infrequently at each other's homes.

I recall thinking that my siblings and I had all done considerably well for ourselves despite our childhood. We all made special contributions to our communities and the country. My sister Elaine returned to college with three small boys, graduating magna cum laude and worked with severely handicapped individuals. She did that for thirteen years until she was subjected to burnout. She kept up this work by becoming involved with the Special Olympics.

To show love and respect for her at the time of her passing, the streets of Adams were lined with handicapped children and friends, each person holding a single rose. They were lined along the street from the funeral parlor to the church. There was not a dry eye as the procession passed by.

George was trained as a tool and dye maker. He progressed to become a vice president of a large tool and dye machine shop, which specialized in manufacturing aircraft engine parts. His ingenuity is acknowledged throughout the industry. Some of their clients included General Electric and Pratt & Whitney. My sister Theresa's secretarial skills allowed her to become a private secretary to various company presidents, and finally she became an administrative secretary in the New York State Prison system.

The staff at the hospital provided outstanding support to my family members while providing outstanding care to me. They were liberal in allowing visitors to see me in the ICCU room. I am thankful for that, and I know my family is appreciative of their courtesies.

On Saturday, July 7, Val's brother, George; his wife, Marie; and his two sisters had their last visit with Val since they had to return to their homes in New England. The house seemed very quiet and empty despite the children still being with me. I had a quiet visit with Val at 8:00 p.m. When I was ready to leave, Val stopped me to ask me if I would come back in the morning to see him after church, before I went home. I assured him I would visit him at around 8:00 a.m. or shortly after because I wanted to go to 7:00 a.m. Mass.

On July 7, my family returned to their homes in New England, and my spirits were diminished. I was subject to some revealing developments during my hospital stay. I mean that in the literal sense. After the respirator was removed, and as I became more aware and somewhat coherent, I discovered that I was completely naked! I would have liked even an ounce of modesty with which to leave the hospital. Forget that.

The ICCU had large window walls to look into the patients' rooms for monitoring from the nurse's station. This meant that everyone who passed by my room got an eyeful. A small washcloth replaced Adam's fig leaf. After a while, I got immune to immodesty by looking the other way. The exposure of notoriety as I was weighed twice daily, once in the morning and again in the evening, was something I could have done without. Both morning and evening performances were performed for the audience's viewing pleasure. Thinking back, I should have charged admission to deter the medical expenses!

Since I could not get out of bed, I was weighed on what I refer to as a "fish scale." A long, flat, rectangular pan was slid under my body and then lifted up to measure my weight. I must have looked spectacular since my arms and legs did not fit on the metal plate; they just dangled to the sides. Spectators watched and laughed. After a few days, someone finally decided to close the blinds on the window to allow me some privacy and to put an end to the crowds gathered outside my room window. I half expected my picture to appear in a well-known magazine, knowing that I looked at least as good as Burt Reynolds!

PRAY FOR ME

Sunday morning, I awoke at 6:00 a.m. I felt well rested, and after attending Mass at 7:00, I went to the hospital just as I had assured Val the previous night. At the hospital, there were two sets of double doors. I approached the second set of doors to enter the intensive care unit.

A well-groomed, dark-haired woman stopped me, asking, "Excuse me, do you have someone in here?"

I answered her, "Yes, my husband, Val." She then asked me about the visitation policies in the intensive care unit. I told her, "It is regular visiting time now, and I just go in, and if it is not possible for me to visit with Val, they simply ask me to wait in the waiting room. The nurses are very good about letting you know when it is okay to visit." I placed my hand on her arm and said, "I hope all goes well with you today."

She replied, "I hope all goes well with you today too."

With that, I told her our family was witnessing a miracle and it was beautiful what had taken place that week. She informed me her husband was there, and she asked if I would please pray for them. I said yes, took a pad from my purse, asked for their names, wrote them down, and then placed the pad back into my purse.

I continued through the doors, not knowing what she did or where she went from that point. I could see Val was sleeping through the glass window, so I sat down in a white leather chair across from his room and watched for him to wake up. I saw Dr. McLaughlin come in, speak to a nurse, and he noticed me sitting in the chair, so he came over to let me know about Val's condition and what treatment they were planning for Val. He asked me if I had any questions, and I smiled and said, "No, thank you, but I want to tell you how much I appreciate the wonderful care he is receiving." He smiled back at me, returned to the desk, and sat down.

When it did not appear to me Val would wake up soon, I walked to the nurse's desk to leave a message for Val. I said, "When he wakes up, please tell him I was here and will return for the next visiting time."

She replied to me, "You may wake him up if you want to."

I told her, "No, I do not want to wake him."

She insisted, "Go ahead; it's all right for you to wake him."

Again, I told her, "No, I do not want to wake him."

Then Dr. McLaughlin said, "Go ahead and wake him up; he will go back to sleep."

Again, I said, "No, I really don't want to wake him up." I thought in my own mind and believed that sleep was the best remedy for anyone with an illness. As I started to leave and pass by Val's room, I had an eerie, strange urge to go in and wake him up, but then I felt panic and fear.

My thought was, *Lord, I knew I would be called on to do your will for a miracle. I just did not know what it would be. Now, I know I should go home and pray for the couple who asked me to pray for them. You told Peter when the cock crowed he would have denied you three times. Three times now the nurse and the doctor have told me to go and wake Val up, and so I related what you told Peter to myself.*

I quickly went home and told my children, "I know what my mission will be from now on. It will be to pray for people who ask me to pray for them." I explained to the children what had happened at the hospital. I invited them to come into the living room to pray with me and that it was okay if they chose not to join me. I can remember some friends of my son were there and they went outside; however, my children joined me in the living room. We all knelt down on the floor in a circle and prayed together.

Later, when I visited Val, upon entering, he pointed his finger at me with his voice strained and said, "Why didn't you wake me up this morning?"

I said, "I told you that you are not number one in my life anymore, and I had to go home and pray for someone who asked me for prayers."

Still in a strained voice and pointing to himself, he insisted, "You pray for me."

I said, "I do pray for you. I must listen and be obedient to our Lord, Jesus, and I am sorry you are upset."

He then added, "I know you prayed for Al Jones, the man in the next room."

I had not realized that the man's name I wrote down was actually Al Jones. I could not understand how Val would have known that, so I asked him, "Val, how do you know that? I did not tell anyone specifically who it was I wanted to pray for."

Val replied, "Val, told me."

I said, "No, he couldn't have told you because he hasn't been here since yesterday."

I then noticed tears run down his cheeks, and he turned his head away from me. How did he know the man's name? I had my doubts about what room the man was in. Before I could discuss this any further with Val, I was requested to leave the room while the respiratory therapist suctioned Val's lungs.

As I was standing in the hallway, a woman who I never saw before approached me and identified herself as being from St. Mary's Church. She was aware that Val was Catholic. She said she was a Eucharistic minister and asked if he would like to receive communion. I replied, "I don't know, but I will ask him just as soon as I can go back into the room."

As the nurse indicated it was all right to go back in, I got as far into the room as the doorway and noticed Val was pointing his finger toward the glass window. I asked him if he needed the nurse. He shook his head no and kept pointing his finger toward the glass. The only other person standing there was the minister. I asked, "Do you want to see her?" He nodded yes. I thought to myself, *Why would he want to see her? Who does he assume she is? Does he think she is his mother, aunt, or other relative who is deceased?* I started to wonder again if he was of sound mind given the fact he had sustained such a high fever recently.

He was in fact pointing to the woman who had identi-fied herself to me as being Margaret, the Eucharistic min-ister from St. Mary's Church. Margaret soon understood that her presence being requested of Val through the glass, and she came closer to me. As we entered further into his room, Val said, "Usually a man with a beard comes to see me from St. Mary's Church."

Val received Communion, and then Margaret said she would like to talk with me in private. We walked out into the hallway, and she asked me, "How did he know I was from St. Mary's? Did you tell him?"

I said, "I have no idea. Besides, how could I? I was near you the whole time. I am just as mystified as you."

So then, she asked me, "How do you pray?" I asked her why she wanted to know. She replied, "You look and show a beautiful faith, something that I have been searching for many years for myself because I am afraid to die. How do you get this faith?"

I said, "I don't know what you see, but I don't make praying complicated. To me, God is very simple, and I just talk and pray to him in an uncomplicated manner."

She smiled, saying, "I think I will try that," and left.

The rest of the day was quiet with Val's usual visitors coming. During one visit, our sons brought the Sunday newspaper in for their father, and it was nice to see him interested in the news outside the walls of the hospital. Later, a young girl was sitting in the chair in the hallway, and Val told me to go out to her and tell her Al Jones would be all right. I went to her, knelt down beside her, and said, "Forgive me, my husband wants me to tell you not to worry and that he is going through the same procedure." She looked in the direction of Val's room and saw him smile and wave at her. She waved in return. When I stood up to go back into Val's room, I was astonished to see Darla Jones emerge from the room next to Val's. It was indeed Al Jones in the room next to Val's, and the subject never came up in conversation between Val and me again.

On Monday the ninth, I was at the hospital with our son Val very early since we were not certain what time Dr. Gentry would arrive. I am unsure of the time when I saw Dr. Gentry enter the critical care unit. He waved to me and asked, "How's our miracle man?"

I replied, "I'm waiting for you to tell us."

He told me he would be in to see us shortly. He wanted to look at Val's chart. It had only been a week since Dr. Gentry left for vacation, and he did not expect Val to be there when he returned. Dr. Gentry politely asked me to leave so he could examine Val, but he asked if our son would stay and help him. At this point, I still had time to make it to Mass at 8:00 a.m., so I went to church. I got home about 9:30 a.m. Our son, Val, said Dr. Gentry was amazed to see Val still alive.

As I began to get ready to go see Val for the evening visiting hours, the telephone rang. It was Dr Gentry. He said, "Mrs. Bouchard, I am getting ready to go in and see Mr. Bouchard. I do not have time to talk to you now; however, I wanted you to know that I have arranged for the University of Alabama in Birmingham to admit him to the hospital. We want to see if they can be of any help to Mr. Bouchard."

I got so scared, my heart started to pound and I shook all over. I was all alone at the time and just didn't know what to do as Val couldn't even be moved for an X-ray, so how in the world would he get transported to another hospital? Since Tom, our dear friend, had been such a spiritual supporter to me during this entire ordeal, I felt the need to talk to him about this new revelation.

Tom was out of his office and was not available at that time. All that I could find out was that he was in New Jersey on business at the Ramada Inn for a meeting with a Dr. Gupta. Through information, I was able to get the telephone number of the Ramada Inn. I spoke to a young man, and I told him it was urgent for me to talk to Tom D'Muhula. The young man informed me that he did not have a reservation for a Tom D'Muhula, although he had a reservation for Dr. Gupta, who had not checked in yet. I then asked the young man to page Tom over the hotel intercom system to see if he was there.

Lo and behold, Tom picked up the telephone. He was shocked that I had found him.

I explained when I called his office, his secretary had said that I might be able to reach him at this hotel. He replied, "It's a miracle you reached me because I am not staying here. I'm taking a bus to the convention center for a meeting and only came inside this hotel to use the restroom before getting back on the bus when I heard my name being paged. So tell me. What's the problem? Is Val worse?"

I told him, "No, but the doctor wants to send him to the University of Alabama Hospital and see if they can help him."

Tom said, "That's great. It may be the Lord wants a medical miracle to happen."

I responded, "Oh, I never thought of it that way. I feel much better now after I've had this chance to speak with you. I hope your meeting goes well and you have a safe trip home. I will be talking to you soon."

On Monday, July 9, Dr. Gentry came into my room in the late afternoon. He hurriedly entered, and I became excited because I thought something was wrong. I felt strange when my heart would pound fast and skip a beat. Immediately, I wanted to call Marie, and before he could say anything, I asked him to send for her, and the doctor said he had already talked to her.

Dr. Gentry took my hand, and I became scared and afraid that the conversation might be like the last time he held my hand, which was doomsday, good-bye. *Oh God, please not again! Let me die in peace.* Dr. Gentry must have known how tense and frightened I was. He asked me to calm down and listen. It was very difficult for me to relax and be able to hear what the doctor had to say. I thought that the information from the daily blood samples, strip charts, and the other monitoring information from the day was going to be bad news. I was expecting the worst! However, I soon realized that the doctor came to talk to me about transferring to Alabama University Hospital (UAB). Again, I needed to focus and regain my composure.

He reviewed my physical condition and emphasized there was nothing further that Methodist Medical Center could do for me to further my recovery. I was indeed fortunate that they were able to stabilize my condition but was warned that I could not remain in this condition for long. I needed further medical attention of the utmost expertise. This was my only hope! He did not know how and was quite astounded that I had survived that long in my condition.

Dr. Gentry explained that he consulted with a fellow alumnus from Duke University. Cardiologist Dr. Whitlow, now at UAB, agreed to accept me as a patient. There were no promises or guarantees that he would be able to save me. Dr. Gentry watched me carefully for my reactions and kept reminding me that I must listen and understand everything he was saying. I understood that my present condition left me with no other options. As the future would hold, my family and I will be ever thankful for this opportunity. At this point, it was arranged that I would be transported via ambulance to McGhee Tyson Airport for transport aboard UAB air medical jet. The day was set for Wednesday, July 11, 1984. Would I see my family again after that? God had blessed us, and possibly he would not bring me this far and not all the way.

It was six in the evening when Val and I discussed Dr. Gentry's proposal about going to the University of Alabama Hospital in Birmingham. Dr. Gentry's idea was that the hospital would evaluate Val's condition and determine the best possible choices for treatment, if any. Val said, "I can't go on the way I am, that's for sure." He then asked me to get in touch with his friends Bob and Gene so that they would come to the hospital and Val could talk to them.

I said, "I don't think the hospital staff will allow them in to see you."

Val said, "You have a lot of people that you can talk to,

and now I need someone to talk to. Don't worry; they can be my other brothers, and they will let them see me."

He also brought up the subject of our wills. He asked me if I thought we could get things in order before he left for Alabama. I said to Val, "I don't know how we can do that since you will be leaving early Wednesday morning. We only have tomorrow, and it will be difficult to get any lawyer to see me on such short notice."

He said, "Well, at least try."

So I replied, "Okay, now I will get in touch with Bob and Gene for you, and I will stay with Joan until Bob comes back home. Then I will come back to see you."

While I was with Bob's wife, Joan, I told her what Val wanted with the wills and that I was unsure if anything could be done on such short notice.

Joan said, "Let me call a lawyer in town that I once used."

I asked, "But it's 7:00 p.m. now, and who would be in their office at this time?"

She said, "Well, they might have an answering service."

I could not believe it when Joan called the lawyer's office to find his secretary was working late that evening. When I spoke to her and explained the predicament we were in, she said she would see what she could do. Almost immediately, the lawyer called me back at Joan's. He told me to meet him at his office at seven the next morning with the wills.

I left Joan and Bob's house at seven forty and went back to the hospital to see Val. He said he had a good visit with Bob and Gene but did not indicate what they discussed. I let Val know I would be meeting a lawyer in the morning. He told me that it made him feel better because he wanted all his affairs to be in order and know that I would be protected should things not turn out well. As I was ready to leave, Val asked me to make arrangements for the priest to come the next morning so he could receive Communion. I kissed Val good night and told him I hoped we would both get a good night's sleep after all the excitement of the day.

The next morning, I met with the lawyer to go over the wills. The lawyer told me to return at 11:00 a.m. He thought the wills would be ready then for Val and me to proofread, and if they were in order, we could sign them in the hospital that afternoon. After leaving the lawyer's office, I decided to stop at the hospital and see Val. I told him about the arrangements I made with the lawyer.

Before leaving to go to church, I asked him if he had received Communion yet. He said no. I told him I probably would not see him after church, but rather after I went to pick up the wills at the lawyer's office at eleven. After Mass, I went to the priest to ask him if he would see Val at the hospital. He said that he would try without making a firm commitment. When I arrived home after church, I called Joan. I told her Val wanted to see the priest that morning, but the priest said to me he was unsure if he could make it or not, due to his schedule. Joan then suggested that I call Father Sweeney.

We oftentimes attended his churches since he was pastor of five missions in the area at the time. When I called him, he said he would be delighted to come and he would be there at 2:00 p.m. I returned to the lawyer's office. He said if there were no other changes, then he could meet me at the hospital with Val to sign them at 3:00 p.m. I could not believe how smoothly everything was falling into place. At 2:00 p.m., Father Sweeney came to see Val. Father Sweeney set up an altar on the tray stand, offered us both reconciliation, read from the Bible, and Val and I received Communion together. It lasted approximately twenty to twenty-five minutes. Father Sweeney wished us well and told us he would pray for us. He touched Val's arm and said, "You are a good man, Val." I thought to myself, *What simple, perfect words he chose to leave with Val.*

At 3:00 p.m., the lawyer arrived at Val's room with two staff members and a nurse who witnessed the signing of our wills. Now, we felt everything was in order. God surely was looking out for us. I didn't think this could have been accomplished in just one day.

Val gave me instructions on some articles he wanted me to bring to him in the morning before leaving for UAB. He wanted a few personal grooming items and a pair of undershorts. I said to him I didn't think they would allow him to wear them because I was told not to bring anything for him. He had been naked under the bed sheets since he was admitted into the emergency room on July 1. He angrily said to me, "I don't give a darn. I'm not going naked. I do not want to be found naked in the woods somewhere if the plane crashes." I got a good laugh out of it although Val was serious about what he said and did not find it funny at all.

Wednesday, July 11

Dear Marie,

It was good of you to call me this morning. When you had told me that Val was sitting up and reading Sunday and was hoping to go home Monday and the phone was so bad I couldn't understand all you were trying to tell me, I said I would call you at night.

Well, I had planned to call you tonight, for I felt I could know by that time how things turned out.

Thank you for calling me this morning. I want to say again that your faith is something beautiful to behold, and almost saintly I feel, and I feel privileged to have you share it with me.

I feel now that the aneurysm was probably the cause of the original heart attack, and while the drugs and other medication may have saved him it was still there.

The care and treatment seems to have built up his physical condition so that now he can stand the angiograph (spelling?), and it will enable them to locate the aneurysm. Then I assume there will be a arterial graft, a bypass operation to restore blood flow to the heart.

All we can do now is hope and with faith that all will go well. As I wrote before, my prayers will be that the doctors and nurses will be granted the skill and knowledge to, and with your faith, that all will go well.

Bypass surgery is considered common today and risk is not considered great, but that is easily said and doesn't ease our concern. All we can do is wait and with your faith and love all will be well.

My love and my "prayers" will be with you all the way and I'll be waiting for good news.

Love,

Dick

"If a man does not keep pace with his companions, it maybe because he hears a different drummer. Let him step to the music he hears however measured or far away."

Henry David Thoreau

NO DOPAMINE

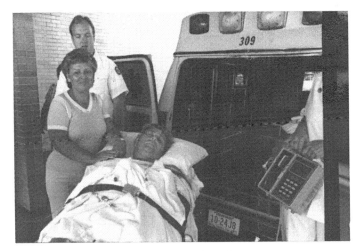

Being transported to airport

Early in the morning on Wednesday, the mood was solemn as an ambulance backed up to the hospital emergency room entrance. A medical team from UAB stepped out, rolled out a stretcher loaded with equipment on it, and headed for Val's room. A woman from the team came to me and said, "This packet of instructions will let you know exactly where your husband will be at UAB." She informed me how they were going to transport Val to the hospital by flying him from Knoxville to UAB on the hospital's medical jet. Due to limited space on the jet, I would need to find my own transportation to the hospital.

Many people gathered at the hospital to see Val leave. I was especially surprised to see Joan since she had a very difficult time going to hospitals ever since her mother passed away. Joan handed me an envelope and said, "I want you have this." I started to cry as I put the envelope in my purse.

Joan and I went back to my house after they took Val to the airport. The morning was beautiful with the sunshine. By the time we arrived at the house, it had become cloudy, and soon it began to pour down at the same time the sun's rays penetrated some patchy clouds, which were reflecting on our rear deck.

As Joan sat at our kitchen table drinking her coffee, I slid open the sliding glass doors that led to our rear deck. I passed through the doors, stepped out into the rain, lifted both my hands up in the air, and said, "Lord, bless me with your holy water from heaven."

Joan looked at me, laughed, and said, "You nut."

By midday, I felt so tired—too tired even to think I could make the trip to Birmingham. I was able to call Val's doctor who would be caring for him, and I asked him to ask Val directly if it would be all right for me to come the next day. The doctor let me know it would be fine for me to do that, and he reminded me of the time difference as being one hour earlier in Birmingham. I said, "Oh, Joan, I am so glad I don't have to leave today. I am exhausted."

Joan said, "It's all going to be okay, Marie. I'm going home now, but I will talk to you before you leave tomorrow."

I said, "Thanks for everything, Joan. I don't know what I would do without friends like you." I did not know how long I would be in Birmingham, so I probably packed more than I needed that night.

My good friend Marge and I arrived in Birmingham at 5:00 p.m. We decided to get a place to stay before going to the hospital. We checked into a hotel, got the room key, and started to walk out when Marge asked the receptionist, "Where do we park our car?"

The girl's answer was, "Around the corner in a lot surrounded by a chain link fence."

Marge then asked the girl, "Is there a lot of vandalism to cars here?"

She replied, "Yes."

We decided this was not where we wanted to stay and cancelled the room. Marge and I left, and I asked her, "What are we going to do?"

Marge simply said, "We'll find another place."

So we drove about one block, saw a hotel, and Marge said, "Let's try there." We parked the car and started to walk toward the hotel entrance, and I looked up and realized it was the Hilton Hotel we were about to enter. I thought to myself, *What does she think I have? This is one of the most expensive hotels there is here. I don't think I can afford for us to stay here.* I said to Marge, "You will have to do the talking to the desk clerk. I can't."

When we approached the desk, Marge asked, "Do you have special rates for people who have family as patients at UAB?"

He answered, "Yes, do you have a card like this?" He held a card up in his hand for us to see. He went on to say, "If you don't have one, you can get one at the hospital."

Then Marge asked, "What are the special rates?"

The man said, "Twenty-six dollars with daily maid service and twenty-one dollars with maid service once a week." I thought, *How good can it get?* I felt like I was dreaming. The rate was a third of what it would have been at the other hotel, and we were getting a double room. We looked at each other and smiled. We had a hard time containing the excitement.

After we registered and got the room key, the man said, "Show your key at the garage entrance. You can park on the sixth floor where your room is located." All we had to do was walk out the hotel entrance and walk a straight line directly to the hospital. It was a short five-minute jaunt from my hotel room to Val's room in the hospital.

Once I entered the hospital, I was astonished both at the size and the absolute cleanliness of the interior. Everything sparkled and smelled so clean as I knew a hospital should look and feel. I entered Val's room, and after a quick embrace, Val whispered to me that the cardiologist wanted to meet with us as soon as I arrived. The nurse paged the doctor for us, and Dr. Whitlow came to explain the first thing he needed to do for Val was an angiogram in order to determine the extent of the damage to his heart.

We were made aware of the very dangerous risks involved in this type of procedure; however, the angiogram would help the doctor decide the best possible treatment available. He then indicated the procedure would be scheduled for the following Monday. Coumadin is a blood thinner, and for the blood to coagulate after the procedure, Val needed to be off this medication and have another medication started, both for a time prior to the angiogram on Monday.

Val was very tired, and he wanted to get some rest. Marge and I were also very exhausted from our trip. We planned then to get dressed up and go have dinner at the hotel restaurant. I mentioned to the hostess of the restaurant that if our hotel room got a telephone call while we were enjoying our dinner, I would appreciate it if she could inform me because it would be from the university hospital. Marge and I relaxed, ate our dinner, and we laughed a little as we conversed. By 10:00 p.m., we decided it was time to go to bed.

Upon entering our room, the first thing we noticed was the flashing red light on the telephone. I asked Marge, "Would you please get the message? It will be the hospital." The message Marge retrieved was from Val, who left a telephone number for me to call him back.

I could hardly believe my ears when I heard Val answer the telephone, whispering to me, "Hello, honey. Tomorrow at 1:00 p.m."

I answered him, "Okay, honey, good night." I placed the telephone back. Right away, I said to Marge, "Can you believe it, Marge? The angiogram is on for tomorrow at one o'clock."

Suddenly, I realized I was not as tired as I had been upon entering our room. Therefore, I decided to open the envelope my friend Joan had handed me the day before. Among the items in the envelope were three prayer cards. One was "The Power of Prayer," another one was "Perfect Trust," and the third one was "Compensation." Something made me turn the "Perfect Trust" card over to look at the back of it to find a prayer handwritten about releasing the souls in purgatory. After reading that, it gave tremendous comfort with the guilt I felt from having not been able to pray for my own husband on July 1. The guilt lifted immediately.

On Friday, July 13, Marge and I went to the hospital, and it seemed like forever before we received any news that the angiogram had proceeded without any problems. Upon getting the information, Marge and I went onto a terrace to give thanks and praise to God for Val having gone through the procedure without any difficulty. It was a beautiful day outside, and as I raised one arm up to the sky, Marge quipped, "You can't praise the Lord with just one hand!" So I put my purse down on the ground, raised both my arms stretched out to the sky, and said, "Praise and thanks be to God!" Marge was happy to take a picture of me praising the Lord. In fact, she even had me sign the pictures she took!

Praise the Lord

Saturday, July 14, Val got out of bed for the first time in a long while. He had been in bed for two weeks without being able to sit up by himself. It was painful for me to watch him take just two steps as it was such a struggle for him and for him to get himself back into his bed. Val had lost a considerable amount of weight in a short period, which contributed a great deal to his weakness.

Dr. Kirkland and his assistant, Dr. Sears, visited Val and me. They were there to explain the results of the surgery and tests performed on Friday. The news was bleak as he went on to say the tests indicated severe damage to Val's heart. Dr. Kirkland said his options were limited to either stay the way he was, with 20 percent of his heart functioning, or to receive a heart transplant with the realities of the transplantation procedures.

Val said, "I certainly do not want to stay the way I am. I don't know much about your profession, but why isn't bypass surgery an option?"

Dr. Kirkland answered, "Because you have been on Dopamine for too long. If we were to discontinue the medication, your heart would stop, and we wouldn't have a way to restart it."

Val replied, "I am not on Dopamine."

Dr. Kirkland replied, "That's impossible. If it was discontinued, you wouldn't be here right now."

I then said, "We have been witnessing a miracle taking place here." Neither Val nor the doctor were pleased with my statement.

Val snapped back, "Never mind what God is going to do with me. I want to know what the doctor is going to do."

Dr. Kirkland instructed Dr. Sears to make sure no Dopamine was being administered to Val. Dr. Sears checked the records and told Dr. Kirkland that no Dopamine was being given to Val. Dr. Kirkland looked at me with an inquisitive expression on his face and then said to Val, "Before we decide anything, I am going to have you moved to a different floor that will give you time to gain some strength. The way you are right now, you would not be able to withstand any kind of surgery. I will not give you an answer tomorrow because this will be one of the most difficult decisions I have ever had to make."

On Sunday, July 15, I was shocked to hear Val tell me they gave him a real bath. He even got his hair washed for the first time in a long time. He had only had those dry shampoos since he was in the hospital in Plymouth, so this was a real treat for him.

Being an engineer, he never stopped looking to see how things were designed. After only five minutes in the tub, he figured out that someone, at some point, would be sitting in the tub and the door would fly open. He realized the door latch was not properly installed on the door, and he brought this to the attention of the person bathing him. He was told that they had the tub for a long time and nothing like that had ever happened before. As fate would have it, when Val was being bathed, the door became unlatched. Water was spilling out all over the floor, out into the corridor, and the nurses scurried to get towels and whatever they could to clean the water off the floor. Val sat there and said, "Would someone please get me a towel?" He later drafted a detailed design of the hospital's bathing tub to illustrate the flaw in the design.

In the days that followed, Val was eating as often as he possibly could, despite his lack of an appetite. He was on a special diet, which presented him with several meals a day so he could regain some strength. His diet also included high-calorie milkshakes.

As time passed and we waited for Dr. Kirkland's decision, Val's appearance changed with each passing day. He began to gain strength and looked healthier to me. On Saturday, July 21, Dr. Kirkland informed us of his decision to do bypass surgery; however, Val still had an extremely high risk of not surviving the surgery. Val was very pleased with the doctor's decision. He understood the risk involved and felt this was a viable option for himself. Val knew in his own heart and mind he could not continue the way he was.

Our friends Joan and Bob arrived on Saturday, and the first thing I said to Joan was, "Why did you give me the prayer card with the prayer on the back handwritten in your handwriting for the souls in purgatory?"

She answered, "I didn't. I was not aware of any prayer on the back of any of the cards."

I told her I had received great comfort with the cards she gave me; however, I received the greatest comfort in reading the handwritten prayer about releasing the souls in purgatory on the back of the one titled "Perfect Trust." I went on to explain the guilt I had carried about having not been able to pray for Val on July 1. The guilt had vanished. I also told her I was only able to pray for the souls in purgatory on that day.

Tuesday evening, the twenty-fourth, Bob and Joan returned to UAB to be with me while Val underwent surgery the next day. They brought with them a witty cartoon depicting Val in terrific likeness to him, made by a fellow worker, signed by all the people in his office, and beautifully framed. The illustration showed a doctor standing next to a hospital bed with Val propped up in it. The doctor said to him, "I have some good news and some bad news. The good news is, you are doing great. The bad news is, we got your chart mixed up with another patient and you've just had a complete hysterectomy." This was just what we all needed, a good laugh.

Joan also brought a Polaroid camera to take some pictures of all of us. I asked Joan if she would leave the camera with me. Bob and Joan left the hospital at 10:00 p.m. I remained with Val until around midnight. Before I left, I asked Val if there was anything he would like us to discuss before his surgery in the morning. Val's reply was, "Anything that needed to be said or should have been said was all said a long time ago." That was a beautiful thing for him to have told me. I was happy to know there would not be anything left unsaid in case there was a negative outcome.

On July 25, I took six Polaroid pictures of Val before he went into surgery. He looked so healthy that it was difficult to comprehend the idea of him requiring such a risky surgery. Dr. Whitlow came into Val's room prior to the surgery, and said, "Val, if I were to put a suit on you and sit you in the hallway, no one would know how sick you really are."

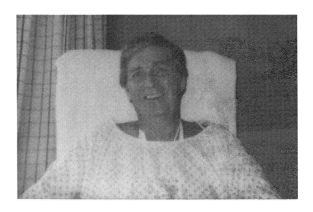

Before surgery at 9:05 a.m.

One picture was for our two sons. Three of the others were for Val's brother and his two sisters with the caption, "If things do not turn out the way we would like, I thought you might like to see a picture of your brother and how he looked just before going into surgery." One picture was for Dr. Gentry, who had arranged for Val to come to the University of Alabama hospital and make it possible for him to have this opportunity. The caption went something like: "Dear Dr. Gentry, I am sending you this picture of how Val looks at 9:05 a.m. the morning of July 25, less than one hour before surgery. Notice how good he looks. You have gone above and beyond your medical profession, and I want to thank you now for all you have done in case things don't turn out the way I'd like for them to."

At ten in the morning, they placed Val on a gurney and wheeled him into the hallway to wait to proceed with surgery. Val said to me, "Good-bye, Marie."

He was emotional, and I asked Val, "What do you mean good-bye? I will see you again soon. God did not bring you this far and then not finish what he started."

On my way to the waiting room, I mailed all the pictures. There were many people in the waiting area. Joan was with me, and Marge stayed in prayer at a different location. We had to sign into this area and were not permitted to leave until surgery was complete. At some point, a hostess called my name. I responded, and she informed me the surgery was over and the doctor was optimistic. She explained the first graft turned the front portion of his heart pink. She went on to tell me as soon as they finish stitching him, they would take me to see him in the recovery area. By this time, Marge had reunited with Joan and me in the waiting area. After some time, the hostess called my name again to let me know the escort service would take me to see my husband.

As we rode the elevator, the escort asked me how I felt, and I responded, "I feel like a bride going to see her groom." When we exited the elevator, there were large doors in front of us, a small waiting area to the left, and we were escorted there. It was just a room without a receptionist or anyone else there. Marge said to me, "Marie, I have some blessed oil. Let's rub some on our hands before we go in and put some on Val." Joan said, "I'll wait here for you because I am not going in."

The doctor came out of the large doors and called, "Mrs. Bouchard." I noticed it was not Dr. Kirkland but his assistant, Dr. Sears. I also noticed that you could not see into the area beyond the two large doors. As the three of us stood there, the doctor said, "Dr. Kirkland is very optimistic. Five grafts were successfully performed on Val. There was a blood clot removed from both the right and left sides of his heart, and there were no aneurysms.

Marge said to me, "Did you hear that? No aneurysms."

I said, "No, all I heard was what he said about the blood clot."

Marge corrected me, "Not blood clot, blood clots." Marge then turned to Dr. Sears and asked him, "Did you say, 'No aneurysms and blood clots'?"

He answered, "Yes." He opened the doors wider and told us we could go in. Marge and I proceeded through the doors while Joan waited outside in the waiting area. The room was circular in design with the nurse's station set up in the middle of the floor. This allowed the nurses to see the patients in their beds with their monitors in stacks on the floor and an attendant beside them, all around the room.

Although I tried not to look up and around the room, I could not help but notice one woman lying in her bed, stark white and struggling to get her respirator off as she moaned and groaned. Right away, I wanted to turn around and leave this place. I continued with Marge, and when we approached Val's bed, I was astonished to see how pink in color he appeared. I felt relieved that Val did not look as frightening after having seen the woman in distress, but I was startled to see all the tubes, the ventilator, and how Val was shivering. They did have a heating blanket on Val, and the heat lamp above him made it very bright. The attendant explained the functions of the monitors stacked next to the bed.

I could not believe Val's pink complexion and the

golden aura around his head. As I was looking at Val, I wanted to believe that I was really seeing what I thought I saw. With a bit of doubt, I turned to Marge and asked her, "What do you see?"

"What do you mean?"

"Tell me how Val looks to you."

Marge said, "He is very pink, and he has a golden glow around his head." We were both very excited and were both rubbing Val with our hands covered with blessed oil. It was so exciting.

Later that evening, Joan's husband, Bob, arrived at the hospital and accompanied me to see Val. Val was sedated quite heavily, so he was not conscious that we were even there. Bob is a big man, so when he saw his buddy laying there with all the tubes and apparatus attached to him, it shook him up and made him alarmed and fearful. Bob had developed his own heart trouble back in 1980, so this made him decide he didn't want to find himself in that situation ever, so he immediately resolved to take better care of himself.

On Thursday, July 26, I went to visit Val at ten in the morning. I was informed I should go downstairs and wait for them to remove the respirator and move Val into a private room. After this was all finished, I would be permitted to go see him. The next day they got Val out of his bed, and I took a picture of him walking down the hallway assisted by a nurse. Exactly forty-four hours after his surgery, he was up and about!

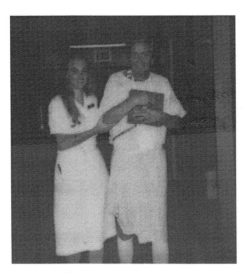

Forty-four hours after surgery

Early in the afternoon, on Tuesday, July 31, I approached Val's room to find the door closed. I knocked on his door and was pleasantly surprised to see that it was Dr. Gentry who opened the door.

I said, "Dr. Gentry, what are you doing here?"

He said, "I couldn't believe what I was hearing about Val, and my wife and I were in the vicinity and wanted to stop by. I talked to Dr. Whitlow about what was going on, and the picture you sent to me made me all the more curious. I think Val looks great! I look forward to seeing him back in Oak Ridge."

I said, "Dr. Gentry, I never asked any questions during the time Val was in the hospital in Oak Ridge."

He said, "I know, and we thought it was unusual."

I replied, "But I must ask you one question now. Why did you call and talk to Val, even though he couldn't respond, on July 5 from your parents' home in Virginia Beach?"

Dr. Gentry looked down at the floor, and he said, "It was God, I guess." Then he lifted his head, looked at my eyes, and he said, "No, it was God." We continued to visit with each other on a level that was more personal.

Dr. Kirkland, the heart surgeon, visited Val Tuesday evening to explain to him that he was going to discharge him soon. He also informed Val that the pharmacist would come see him about the medication that he would need to continue with at home and about his follow-up visit with the cardiologists in Oak Ridge.

I said, "Dr. Kirkland, I want to thank you for everything you have done for us. I can't tell you how much it is appreciated."

Dr. Kirkland asked me, "Why are you thanking me? You knew it was going to be all right because you told me." What a profound statement I found that to be. Val wanted to know what the outlook was, and Dr. Kirkland told him he could expect to get about two to three years with the reparation he performed.

BACK TO WORK

On Wednesday, dear friends of ours, upon hearing of Val's medical condition, drove all the way from Pennsylvania to Birmingham to see us. Connie was a young girl when she first worked for Val and he took her under his wing. Her family sincerely appreciated everything he did for their young daughter, and they became close friends. Her mother, Lois, accompanied Connie to see Val.

On August 2, Val was discharged from the hospital. How secure and fortunate Val and I felt to have Connie and her mother following behind us in their vehicle back to our home in Oak Ridge. As we drove into the subdivision, we saw big yellow ribbons decorating the sign at the entrance to our neighborhood. When we continued onto our street, not far we saw the trees and mailboxes all garnished with yellow ribbons, creating within us an emotional response. With Val's military history, I could vividly recall how the families must have felt when POWs found their way home to their families—awesome and emotional.

The first Sunday we were home, Val went to church. It was August 5. One day, during the following week, Val actually went into the office for two hours. The next couple of weeks included follow-up visits with Val's cardiologist, an exercise regimen, and a sensible diet. Val was very anxious, but he had to wait for the release from the doctors before he could return to his career on a full-time basis.

Arriving home from UAB on August 2 was very emotional. When we turned onto our street, there was a welcome home sign covered with yellow ribbons. As we continued up the street, all we could see were yellow ribbons. It was the yellow ribbons that choked us both up, but when we saw the group of people to welcome us home, that brought on the tears. We had daily visits from many acquaintances and neighbors, and the phone rang constantly.

Dr. Kirkland had contacted Parkway Cardiology and spoke to Dr. McLaughlin about my stay at the UAB Heart Center. An appointment was arranged for the following Monday. Connie and her mother, Lois, stayed with us only a few days before returning to their home in Middletown, Pennsylvania. When they left, it was as if family had departed.

Marie did the answering to the callers and the visitors; I was the quiet one. We wrote thank you letters to many friends and to other patients and their families. It was a busy time, and Marie was not getting any rest. Finally, the welcome-home calls diminished, and we started to return to a more normal life. Marie and I felt good with our first visit with Dr. McLaughlin. We were no longer feeling melancholy as we did when we left the heart center. After such a tremendous experience and anxiety, there was a sense of "letdown" and perhaps even feelings of sadness or disappointment.

We were back, and the walk with the shadow was over.

We had peace of mind and were looking forward to good days. Full of anxiety, of a pleasant nature, the nervousness was still in the background. The good doctor came in and hugged me with the biggest smile. I was like the long lost son coming home. It was such a good feeling for both of us; it is difficult to express our inner feelings because it was good. He went over the discussions with Dr. Kirkland, the parts of the discussions that he wanted to share with us.

The prognosis for the next few years was good, and there were some items in my lifestyle that I would need to change, such as diet, exercise, rest, and realizing my physical limitations. These proved to be difficult in the beginning, but with Marie controlling the menu, it became livable. No more quantities of bacon, sausage, and fried foods, etc. The fast food hamburger restaurants became off limits. I realized that if you do not go in or see it, it stays only in the back of your mind. Ice cream was limited, which was really difficult.

Appointments were set up for monthly visits until I rarely was required to go. The visits went well, and we were pleased. Parkway Doctors McLaughlin, Barry, and Gentry, who saved me from the shadow, and the office staff all met with us briefly in the waiting room. God certainly placed a lot of talent in one place. Dr. Garton would become my family physician, as I never had had a regular doctor. He turned out to be an excellent physician and friend. One more great person in my life.

After Val returned to work, he was able to arrange his schedule and to accommodate a trip to Plymouth. This made it possible for Val to visit Jordan Hospital where he had previously stayed, check on the project's status at the nuclear plant, and have a reunion with his family. He went to the hospital to thank them for all they had done for him while he was a very sick patient in late May to the middle of June. Not only that, he completely stunned the doctor and the nurses when they saw him. With Val's mission accomplished, we returned home to resume a normal life together. We decided then that we would never be separated, and if he had to travel, I would accompany him, when permissible.

Saturday, August 4

Dear Marie,

Your card, letter, came yesterday. It was very thoughtful of you to write.

You seemed to be standing in the room watching me as I read, and when I finished, I was deeply moved and humbled. Being of a practical nature, my prayers were mostly that the doctors and nurses would have the knowledge and skill to take care of his problem, and when I read that the hospital was "known throughout the world for its outstanding heart surgery unit," I felt that my prayers might have been answered. The fact that he arrived at this particular hospital was part of the miracle too.

You were part of the miracle too in the way you stood like a rock in your faith through all the critical weeks.

I'll be waiting to learn how Val stood the trip

home and how he is progressing; tell him I'm thinking of him.

With love,
Dick

September 1984

I made a trip, with Marie, to Plymouth, Massachusetts, where all my problems began. I was able to check on the progress at the Pilgrim Plant, but my main purpose was to thank the wonderful doctor, nurses, and staff who took care of me during our time of crisis. It was important to me to thank them for all they did for me and for the support they gave to my wife. We also made a quick stop at the Governor Bradford Motel for their superior kindness.

Our next stop was Hampden, Massachusetts, where my family had gathered to see us. After a little visit, I was tired, and my brother took me to his bedroom for a rest. I looked at his bed, and for the first time in many months, I enjoyed a full-blown belly laugh. What I saw on his bed made me laugh so hard, it hurt. There was the ugliest man stuffed doll sitting next to an ugly Cabbage Patch doll. It was like nothing I had ever seen before. It was made from silk stockings, with disarrayed black hair and blotches of hair dangling from his armpits and a beer can stuck to one hand. The clothes matched his ugliness. Marie was so happy to see me enjoy the moment that she told my brother to get one for me. We named him Ugly Man. When I would seem to get a little down, Marie would bring the doll out to make me laugh again and cheer me up.

In October, I returned to work full time. I did an

exercise program faithfully on a daily basis. When I traveled, if it was possible, Marie went with me. We decided not to be apart, ever, if it was possible for us to be together.

For the next three years, I made certain I altered our lives in many ways, including but not limited to Val's diet, making sure he got plenty of rest and did his exercise. In February of 1985, we had a celebration-of-life dinner to express our gratitude to our friends and the professionals that we believed went above and beyond their calling in providing us with unending support.

February 1985

We had a celebration-of-life dinner for the people who were among our support system, as well as the physicians in Oak Ridge. It was a joyous evening. Family, friends, and medical professionals all gathered together over dinner, sharing stories, love, and laughter. It was exhilarating. It was such a wonderful celebration of life. To see the physicians with their wives together enjoying a positive moment in their careers was refreshing.

An unusual occurrence took place that same month, February. I received a telephone call from the mortuary that I had made arrangements back on July 2. I was asked what I would like them to do with the death certificate I had partially completed and they still had in their possession. I asked, "What do you usually do with them when a person does not expire and recovers?" I was informed that they sometimes destroyed them since they were not permitted to keep them after six months. I was also informed that sometimes they were returned to the family for them to dispose of the certificate. I then said, "Well then, go ahead and dispose of it in the manner you usually do." Then I said, "No, wait a minute, may I come and get it?" I was told yes, and not knowing why I decided I wanted the certificate, I went by and picked it up.

Summer 1985

Marie and I became involved in the St. Mary's School renovation project. We wanted to give something back for having received a second chance.

1986

I was blessed with attending my son Jim's wedding in Brattleboro, Vermont.

In October of 1987, we were both able to see our first granddaughter, Christine. During the first few months of 1989, we all became aware of the deterioration in Val's health. By April, he was instructed not to lift anything over a few pounds in weight. Realizing this, Val chose to lift his first grandchild up for what he knew would be the last time. In July of 1989, our second grandchild, Christopher, was born.

Val's health continued to decline to the point he required oxygen at various times during the day. No one at his office or within the corporation was aware of the extent of the decline because he was remarkable at concealing how he really felt. He dressed sharp, carried himself in an upbeat fashion, and performed meticulously at his work.

To watch him work was to see him so full of life doing what he loved to do with his mind still working at its fullest potential, but the physical frame that encapsulated him was becoming frail.

I dreaded the nighttime because I loved this man so much. He never complained, no matter how terrible he felt. All our married years, we liked to cuddle when we slept, but I found it more difficult to sleep next to him. He would ask me at night before going to sleep, "Where are you? You're so small. I cannot find you in this big bed. I can't feel you, and I want to touch you." The reason was I was literally hanging off the edge of the bed. I felt so much guilt for thanking God for one more day and never asking for a tomorrow. His hands and his feet were always so cold because of poor circulation, and I could never detect a pulse. I would fall asleep feeling so helpless.

As the months wore on, it made me very sad for us to go on in silence and to make the best of what we had together, but, of course, we had no other choice. It was by far the hardest thing I have ever had to do, night after night. His heart muscle had become so enlarged in his chest cavity, which caused his lungs to become atrophied. This now required Val to need increased amounts of oxygen more frequently and a larger oxygen cylinder than the portable one he had been previously using. It looked so cold and out of place in our bedroom next to our bed.

Val's enlarged heart would at times just stop, and then, with a thud, suddenly kick back and start again. When this happened, he would shake a little back and forth and then settle back down to normal. It was almost like watching an old-fashioned car with a crank start.

1987

Our first granddaughter, Christine Eva, was born, and I got to hold her shortly after her birth—a wonderful feeling that I cannot describe.

Picked up Christine for the last time

Easter, 1989

I picked up my granddaughter for the last time as I was recently told my heart was failing and was told that I should not lift anything over a pound. This was truly heartbreaking for me. I kept a picture of her and me taken that day in my office at work. It was a reminder of how fragile my life was, and seeing her sweet face in the picture gave me comfort.

July 1989

A grandson, Christopher Matthew, was born.

In January of 1990, Val knew the inevitable was closing in on him. He was taking the maximum dosages of his medications, and there was nothing more that could be done for him. He continued not letting anyone know these facts. During the first week of March, Val had his mind made up that he was going on a business trip with Bob to Sacramento for ten days. Bob told Val he did not want him to make the trip without a green light from his doctor. So Val called me on the telephone to let me know about his intentions of going with Bob and asked me to pack a bag for him. When he came home, he made a comment that the doctor had changed his medication.

Keep in mind, I was unaware he had a doctor's appointment. So I asked him, "What medicine did he change?"

Val answered me and said, "My Lasix."

I knew enough to realize that if the dosage he told me was correct that he should be in bed, not traveling. So I suggested I call the doctor to be sure, but Val quickly said, "Oh, no, I can do that." Now, in all of Val's years, he never called a doctor. Right then, an alarm should have sounded in this cuckoo's nest, but it went completely over the tree! If Bob had any idea of the shenanigans his friend managed to pull off, he would have traveled solo without Val.

January 1990

I got the news I did not want to hear. There was nothing more that could be done for me, and I was maxed out on my medications. I didn't tell anyone and kept on working. I didn't want my last days to be spent just waiting for the end. I got involved in a design concept of low-level waste disposal. Although my body was weak, my mind was strong. I was enthused in this project, and working on it kept my mind off my physical problems.

Our son Jim's wife was due to have her first child on March 19. Val wanted me to go and be with her until she had the baby and remain with her for two weeks afterwards. I figured I would be there until the end of March or early April. I really did not want to be away from Val for that length of time. I drove Val to the airport early Wednesday morning to catch a 7:00 a.m. flight to Sacramento. Before I started the long drive to Connecticut, I went to our family physician's office to clarify the change in medication Val talked about the day before. I asked the receptionist if she would ask Dr. Garton about Val's visit and medication change. Dr. Garton heard me and asked to speak to me. He came out into the reception area and asked me, "Did Val go to Sacramento today?"

I said, "Yes."

He said, "Did he tell you that I told him he might die on this trip?"

I said, "No. He left that little detail out, and guess what, Dr. Garton? He is sending me to be with our son and his wife until she has her baby and to care for her and the baby after she comes home from the hospital. I guess nothing else has to be said except that I have a lot of prayers ahead of me."

I got in my car, looked straight ahead, did not look back, and prayed. I drove continuously, with the exception of stopping for gas, to use the restroom, and for coffee. I made it to the New York and Connecticut border by 11:00 p.m. and found a hotel to settle in for the night. I called our home. My daughter-in-law answered the phone, and in the course of the conversation, she said, "Don't hurry. Valarie had a baby girl at 8:00 p.m., and Dad left his number where he can be reached." With that, I breathed a sigh of relief because I knew I would not have to be away from home and from Val longer than two weeks. I placed a call to Val in Sacramento and never mentioned how he had pulled the wool over my eyes.

I arrived late in the morning at the hospital, where our newest grandchild, Bethany Marie, was born. I took a day to have lunch with our friends, Tom and Donna. We had a nice visit, and as we stood outside, before we said good-bye, Tom, aware of Val's deteriorating condition, asked me what I wanted for Val. I said, "First, God's will to be done, and if God wants to touch his heart with his hand and heal it, I know he can, and it is possible for him to give Val a new heart."

Tom then made a notation in his little black notebook and said he would pray for us. Then Tom said to me, "We have a friend, Jane, in Atlanta, who needs a heart transplant. Would you pray for her?"

I said, "I will." With an embrace, we said good-bye and went on about our day.

I spent a week with my children and their baby when Valarie informed me her mother was anxious to come and be with them. It also gave me a reprieve to be able to go home and be with Val, in as much as I would have liked to stay. I called Val to let him know I was coming home.

When I arrived in Bristol, Tennessee, I telephoned Val to let him know I was about three hours away from home and I might be able to make noon Mass. It was the first time he ever told me he was glad because he needed me. For an instant, oh, how I wished I had a jet plane. I know it was prayer that kept me going because, without it, I could've gone absolutely stark, raving mad only wanting to get to my beloved, especially not knowing how his trip was to Sacramento.

March 1990

Another granddaughter, Bethany Marie, was born in Connecticut. Marie was there for this occasion.

May 1990

I asked Marie to drive me to Connecticut so I could see Jim and his little family. Marie was reluctant, but I convinced her. I could never forgive myself if I didn't try, and she gave in. We arrived in Connecticut May 10. We also went to Brattleboro, Vermont, to attend a wedding of Jim's best friend. Jim was in the wedding party, and the couple is Bethany's godparents. We spent the night in a little home in Vernon, Vermont, for the weekend. On Monday, May 13, I made a visit to Vermont Yankee, as usual, trying to drum up some business. The next day we went back to Connecticut to return to Jim's place.

I knew I was failing but wanted to deny that I was

having a struggle. I consumed all my oxygen, and on the eighteenth, I asked Marie if she could call to get my oxygen bottle refilled. She informed me it was not possible without a prescription. I waited for about an hour and then asked Marie to take me to the small community hospital, which was just a few blocks away. Marie said to me, "I wondered how long you were going to put us through this agony before you asked for some help."

The hospital was quiet. There was only one other patient in the emergency room at the time. The physician, first after speaking to each of us, said he was going to admit me to the critical care unit, and since there were no patients in there, they had to get the unit prepared. He said there wasn't much he could do for me, but he would try to make me comfortable and stabilize me. He also said my only hope would be for me to try to get a heart transplant and that I might want to talk to Dr. Kirkland, the doctor who did my bypass surgery. He said he was at UAB a few months ago and met Dr. Kirkland. I spent the night in the ICCU. On May 20, Dr. Kannan came in early in the morning and said he felt I could be moved out of ICCU but not discharged.

He asked me if I would like to be in a room with another patient for some company. He said the man who was in the emergency room the day before had also been admitted but was not as bad off as I was. If it was all right with me, I could be in a room with him. I didn't mind, as it would help to pass the time between visiting hours.

Marie and Jim came during visiting hours and left at the appropriate time. The family of the other patient, his wife and two daughters, stayed because they were worried about him. At around 8:00 p.m., Dr. Kannan made a visit to our room at the end of the visiting-hour period. He tried to suggest to the family of the other patient to go out and get some dinner and then home to get a good night's rest. His family decided it was a good idea and said they would go home after dinner.

Now we were prepared to watch the *Show of Shows with Sid Caesar*. It was very funny, and we were laughing a lot. It was a one-hour show, and sometime during the second half of the show, I heard a strange kind of noise coming from the man in the bed next to mine. I thought to myself, *What a strange laugh,* and looked over at him, and he looked strange. I soon realized something was awry, and, in fact, it looked like he'd expired. I rang for the nurse, and she asked over the intercom, "Yes, can I help you?"

I replied, "No, not me, but the man in the bed next to me. I think he has gone away."

She asked, "Where did he go?"

I answered, "I believe to heaven."

She said, "What do you mean heaven?"

I told her then, "You better come and take a look for yourself!" After she came in and took one look, all chaos broke loose.

I was put in the hallway in a chair. I thought to myself, *I am supposed to be getting better and what a mess.* There was a lot of excitement and emergency personnel running around. This went on for quite a while before I was taken to another room. I was glad to be put in another bed; however, I came to the conclusion I must be having a nightmare, but I knew I was awake. I couldn't believe I was now in a room with an alcoholic experiencing the DTs, yelling and screaming and carrying on. I remember thinking at that moment, *Boy, if I don't die of a heart attack before I get out of here, I'll be lucky.*

When Marie came to visit me later on, she was as white as a ghost. She didn't know I had been moved, and when she went to the room I was in the night before, she saw the room was completely empty. She went scurrying down the hallway to the nurse's station. The nurse told her she was sorry because she was supposed to stop her from going to the room to inform her of my room change. I thanked God the next day after being discharged. I was so thrilled to be headed home to Tennessee.

I had been stabilized enough to make the trip home. Marie and I had committed to putting on a dinner for a young man who was being ordained into the priesthood. We had done a dinner for the same young man when he became ordained as a deacon. At that time, the priest asked us to do the ordination dinner for him, and I said yes. Marie was not pleased because we did not know how I'd be in six months. Well, before our trip to Connecticut, we had all the food ordered and I had people assigned to each task. I went back to work without saying much about my trip to Connecticut. I met with our family physician and the Parkway Cardiology Group. Each said they would see if I could get evaluated at either UAB or Vanderbilt for a heart transplant.

At the church, Marie was preparing some of the food ahead of time for the dinner the next day. When my daughter-in-law called Marie, she informed her that she should call Parkway Cardiology. When Marie called, she was given two dates: one at Vanderbilt and one at UAB for an evaluation. Since Vanderbilt's date was the earliest date, Marie decided we would go to Vanderbilt. Marie called me at my office and told me I should call Parkway Cardiology and confirm the date, which I did. On Friday, May 25, Marie and I went to a reception at Lakeside Grill for our friend's daughter. Although everyone said I looked well, I felt extremely tired.

Reception, May 25, 1990

May 26

I woke up early, and Marie and I went to the church to get the dinner started. Marie had a small cot brought into a small room off the kitchen. She put my oxygen next to the cot and covered it. We tried to conceal how serious my condition really was. At brief periods during the day, I went into the little room to rest and use the oxygen. The dinner went smoothly. It was calm and quiet. Bishop said he wished all the dinners he had to attend were like this one, as it was home cooking, which he enjoyed. We were pleased with his comments. When everything was cleaned up, Marie told me it was time to go home.

The days that followed I could feel myself becoming weaker and weaker, but I continued to work every day. I came home at lunchtime and rested because I didn't feel like eating. I was still waiting for a confirmation date from Vanderbilt. I was very concerned because we already had a confirmation date from UAB but not from Vanderbilt.

Finally, on Friday, June 8, I came home at noon. It was a very restless day for me, and I asked Marie to call Vanderbilt to find out what the delay was. Marie said, "I'm sorry, Val, a date has not been scheduled yet."

I replied, "Oh God, I'll never make it." Marie made the call and told the woman at Vanderbilt who did the scheduling what I had said about not being able to make it.

Faye replied, "If you want to come on the following Wednesday, they can admit you to the hospital. There was not time to schedule an evaluation by the next clinic date."

I was so disappointed and restless for the remainder of the day.

Unbeknownst to me, people from work were calling Marie, as they were concerned about me and expressed to her that I did not look well. I thought I had concealed how I was feeling, but I guess not. On Saturday, I was wishing for the weekend to be over. Sunday morning, Marie and I were ready for church, and I decided to have my son trim my hair. As I sat in the chair, I could sense my sight becoming blurry. I was dizzy and asked for help to the couch so

I could lie down. I then asked Marie to take me to the hospital.

The next thing I knew, someone was rocking me, but I didn't know who. I could hear loud prayers and someone else giving our address. I then asked, "Where am I?"

Marie answered, "You collapsed, and we put you on the floor."

I said to her, "I thought you were taking me to the hospital."

Marie said, "An ambulance will be here shortly to take you."

I told her I did not want to go by ambulance and I wanted her to take me. But she said emphatically, "I'm the boss now, and you must listen to me."

I didn't say any more, and soon I was having needles put into my arm, oxygen put on my face and then being lifted onto a stretcher. When we arrived at the emergency room, a doctor from Parkway Cardiology was waiting for me and immediately gave instructions to everyone what to do. As I lay in the emergency room, I could feel myself fade in and out of consciousness and hear dull voices.

The doctor was giving instructions like a battlefield commander, and everyone was scurrying around with a sense of purpose, and a nurse, whom I knew from Saint Mary's Church, was on duty and was holding my hand. She was talking, but I could not understand her. Another voice was heard saying, "Val, this is Father Chris from Saint Mary's, and I came to bless you and anoint you." It was comforting to me and made me emotional as I thought to myself, *This could be it for me. My walk with the shadow will be over soon.* In previous crises, I was anointed in Plymouth by a lay person in 1984 and received the sacrament of Extreme Unction from Father Bois and subsequently by Father Sweeney. *I will sure get to heaven*, I thought, *because many are not fortunate enough to receive just one blessing.*

I did get emotional; however, I was ready to leave with peace of mind and heart. I don't know where the time went or how long I was in the ER, but Marie told me the next day it was five hours. My potassium was depleted, so I was hooked up intravenously along with morphine since the pain I was experiencing was so severe. I could have never imagined such intense pain. My arm was red, and my arteries appeared white against the redness of my skin, and this seemed to cause the pain and looked very strange to me. I did complain how much this hurt. The morphine medication was increased, and I must have passed out.

Jim had flown down to Tennessee from Connecticut, and he, along with Marie and Val, had visited me during the night. Morning came, and I did not know what had transpired during the night.

When I awoke, I was on oxygen and with no pain. I do not recall much except that this was the day I would go to Vanderbilt. Marie and my two sons were there. Jim said he did visit me after he arrived in Oak Ridge, but I had no recollection of that visit. I felt as though my body was asleep. It was a strange bleak kind of feeling with a question in my mind as to what was really happening. People were in and out of the room. There were times when I could hear my heart beating strong, then nothing until a very rapid beating occurred.

Fatigued, I dropped on the bed and went to sleep. It was as if I passed out. At 3:30 a.m. on Monday, June 11, I awoke feeling completely rested, and my thoughts were of ironing. To this day, I cannot imagine why in the middle of the night I would ever think about ironing when I'd not given such an activity a thought in many months. The ironing basket was overflowing although I was not concerned about it. So I decided to get out of bed and put a dent in that large pile of clothes that needed to be ironed. In fact, there may be an article or two of clothing that we would need if we went to Vanderbilt and especially if we were going to be there for an extended period of time. Before I knew it, it was already 6:00 a.m., and I'd finished the entire pile of clothes. I looked around, and all I could see were newly pressed clothes hanging everywhere. While ironing Val's shirts, I was able to capture some of the aroma of the cologne he had previously worn. This gave me a tremendous sense of his presence, as if he were there with me in the house. I could not help but wonder if Val would ever get to wear any of his shirts again. I took a shower, washed and set my hair, and while I sat under the hair dryer, I said my morning prayers as I often did.

While I dressed for church I could not help but think about what was ahead for Val and me. It was not easy to pass the hospital on my way to church, and I did not stop by the hospital to check the status of Val's condition. Doing that left me with such an empty feeling in my heart.

As I walked into church, I could not contain the hot tears that began to stream down my cheeks as though my eyes were attached to a spigot. I tried hard to hold back the tears, but to no avail. I knelt down on the kneeler to pray, but my concentration was not on our Lord. I asked God to help me give him my attention because I was having a difficult time. I knew my love and prayers had to be for him and for me to abide by his will above all my human feelings. At that moment, I felt a tap on my shoulder from someone in the pew behind me.

It brought me comfort to notice it was Kathy, the nurse from the emergency room at the hospital. She had just completed her night shift and came to Mass in the morning, as she did many times before going home to rest. She said to me, "I just looked in on Val before I left work, and he is hanging in there." At the thought of Val, my heart leapt with joy, and I was able to settle down and give all my attention to our Supreme Being with tremendous gratitude. God was making it quite clear for me, as if to say, "Settle down, girl, and focus your attention on me." This made me chuckle silently.

After Mass, I went directly to the hospital. Val was a very sick man; however, he did look a good deal better than the day before. A nurse informed me that Dr. Lane wanted to see me at the nurse's station. Dr. Lane told me Vanderbilt had a bed available for Val and it would be about two hours before they transferred him to the Medical Center there. I thought, *What a nice opportunity for Val to be taken to the Medical Center at Vanderbilt.*

I hurried home and packed enough casual clothes and dress clothes in case we remained there in Nashville for a long period of time. I was instructed to bring very little for Val because he would not need anything except personal hygiene items. The boys made certain the car was ready for the trip. I had already made reservations for a hotel, and everything was ready. Young Val, Jim, and I returned to the hospital. We all talked and expressed our feelings about what was taking place. Jim said the most considerate words to his father: "Just think, Dad, this may be just the chance for you to be able to dance with Mom again." Jim remembered what his father had said to me back on July 1 in 1984, six years ago.

I reflected back to that morning of July 1 as I lay next to Val. He rubbed my forehead with his fingers, and he said to me, "Do you know what I've been laying here thinking about? When will I ever be able to hold you close to me and dance with you again?" It was such a thoughtful thing for Jim to remember after six years.

Dance

VANDERBILT HOSPITAL

June 11, 1990 - Val asked me if he could be alone with the boys for a few private moments. In the meantime, I went to see if I could sign the discharge papers. The nurse then said to me as I was signing them, "The helicopter has just landed on the pad."

I said to her in response, "What? He's flying?"

She said, "Yes."

I replied to her, "Does Val know?"

She answered, "I don't know."

Well, then, I took off down the hall, opened the door to Val's room, and interrupted his conversation with the boys. I asked him, "Honey, do you know you are going by air ambulance?"

Val answered me, "I am? Thank God!"

I said, "That's nice."

Once again, I was upstaged by our Lord. Every time I make plans, they get changed one way or another. Now I must find my own way to the Medical Center. I had planned to follow the ambulance. I then stated, "The Life Flight helicopter with medical personnel from Vanderbilt hospital just landed on the other side of the hospital."

Val told the boys good-bye so we could have a few minutes alone together before they came to get him to board the helicopter. Val told Jim he might as well return to Connecticut to his family since there was nothing he could do, and he expressed to Jim his appreciation for him coming to see him.

Val then said, "All you can do for me now is pray." The boys indicated to their father that they would wait to say good-bye when they brought him out to the ambulance. The ambulance would carry Val to the helicopter pad located just a block over from the hospital. Val then asked me to bring him a notepad and a pen because he had a few things he wanted me to write down for him.

We kissed and hugged, and I said, "I don't know how much time we have, and I am ready to write down whatever it is you wanted me to write down." Val began to name people to be pallbearers for him.

"How pessimistic can you get?" I blurted. "The audacity of you. If and when it ever becomes necessary for those arrangements to be made, I can do whatever I need to do. I do not need for you to plan it in advance. We should take a minute at a time and see where the path is leading us; we must keep the faith and wait for God's answer."

We heard a knock at the door, and we knew it was time for him to go. Our eyes filled with tears as the flight nurses asked me to leave the room so they could prepare Val for the trip.

A group of well-wishers gathered to see Val off. They were waiting outside, near where the ambulance was, although not too close. As hospital staff wheeled Val to the ambulance just outside, before they lifted him up into the waiting ambulance, he was able to kiss our two grandchildren and our sons good-bye. Then Val waved to the well-wishers, who were waiving back at him. Everyone then walked over to be near the helicopter pad, and so did I. When the ambulance arrived to put Val into the helicopter, I walked alongside the stretcher up to the helicopter. The crowd almost automatically moved away to allow us privacy.

I knew Nashville was west of Oak Ridge. I had nothing but dread at the thought of a three-hour trip by ambulance. This was just another part of the horrible experience. I was thankful when Marie told me that a helicopter ambulance would transport me. My only rides on a helicopter had been from La Guardia airport to the top of the RCA building in New York. Those flights always made me nervous, flying so close to those tall buildings. Taking those flights were a last resort when arriving on flights that were late. This trip I was now about to take gave me no choice. Considering how sick I was, I knew I wouldn't be looking out the window.

The time came, and I was placed in an ambulance for the one-minute ride to the helicopter pad. There were many people gathered to see me off. Val, Jim, and two grandchildren were there. The children were dressed so cute, and I remember trying to smile, but I could not. I couldn't talk or show any emotion; in fact, I felt nothing. My position in the helicopter was feet first, and I was placed to the left side. Oxygen, monitors, etc., were in place and connected to me. Then the door was closed, and the helicopter lifted off within a minute. The nurses talked quietly amongst themselves as they kept watch on my vital signs and monitors. They appeared concerned but acted in a calm and professional manner.

Once we arrived at Vanderbilt Medical Center, I was whisked off the helicopter and rushed inside to an elevator to the seventh floor. I was taken through security doors in the ICCU and placed in a large room surrounded by glass. It was very bright. Medical personnel were there as if they were waiting for me. The first voice I heard was that of a cardiologist who told me his name and that he would be examining me. He gave instructions for raising my potassium level. I could feel the fear and widening of my eyes at the thought of having to go through such agony again. I asked, "Is there a pill or drink I could take instead of the IV?" I was informed there was a liquid, but they said it had not been successful. I asked if they could mix the medication, the potassium, with orange juice and crushed ice.

When the concoction was made, a pan was brought along with it. I asked what the pan was for. I was told that it was for when I threw up; they would be ready and not have a mess to clean up. I held my breath for as long as I could, and I drank and swallowed as fast as I could until the six-ounce glass of liquid was gone. It wasn't that bad as my tongue didn't have time to sense the taste. My throat felt very cold, like it was frozen and it hurt, but I was relieved it was over. I took the medication this way each time until the blood level reached the satisfactory level.

I drifted in and out of consciousness, not knowing what was happening or even how long I was in that state. When I became somewhat aware again, I could feel the oxygen mask was removed and tubes were now in my nose. I wondered just how bad I was and thought to myself, *What a waste to be just a living thing. When one dies quickly, it's a blessing, and the misery and suffering is over.* I just wanted to give up. Then my mind wondered, *When will Marie get here? I need her just to be close.* I kept my eyes closed, wishing to hear her voice and have her hold my hand.

On the third day in the ICCU, I was asked if I would mind having my room changed. This room was large and had the equipment for a young woman who was in critical condition. She was suffering from the same illness that Jim Henson, the founder of the Muppets, had: Group A Streptococcus.

I was surprised with the location of the new room, as it was above the helicopter pad. This gave me an eerie feeling every time I heard the helicopter rev up, ready for another mission, and the same feeling knowing it was always a matter of life or death. These missions continued all hours of the day and night. The door to my room remained closed at all times. It wasn't easy to remain calm at times when a lot of commotion could be heard in the hallway. When a code blue was announced, I knew someone was in deep trouble or had passed away. What a way to hang on; not knowing if I would survive was difficult enough with the added stress of hearing the goings-on in the ICCU as a whole. It was only guesswork on my part as not a word was ever spoken about the other patients. Sometimes I would hear a new patient being admitted, which left me wondering what became of the person who had occupied the room before.

When I was permitted to stay with Val, we could look out the window with a clear view of the helicopter pad below. I watched in amazement as each shift on duty meticulously maintained the Life Flight helicopter and each pilot went over the same maintenance procedures. Each time the helicopter started and flew off the helicopter pad into the air, my heart pounded because I knew it was a matter of life and death. Since this was a hospital with a major trauma center, this was a frequent occurrence. The vantage point gave me an idea of how it was when they wheeled Val in on the stretcher when he arrived on the eleventh.

The next few days Val underwent many tests and procedures as part of the evaluation process. On the evening of June 14, Val sat up in bed reading, and I was sitting in a chair reading. The door suddenly opened, and a young doctor looked at Val inquisitively and asked him, "Are you all right?" Val answered him, "Yes." The doctor closed the door. Val and I glanced at each other with a puzzled look.

He said to me, "I wonder what that was all about."

The door opened again, this time a nurse accompanied by the doctor, and he was asked again, "Are you sure you're all right?"

Val answered, "Shouldn't I be?"

The doctor asked, "Can you hear all the alarms ringing? That's you setting them off." The doctor was surprised Val was sitting up in his bed reading with his blood pressure as low as it was.

Val explained to the doctor that he had experienced low blood pressure for a long time and was adjusted to that condition. The next morning, June 15, after the previous night's episode with Val's monitors, I decided to move to a hotel closer to the hospital because that experience left me feeling uneasy.

On the evening of June 16, I started to feel strange. I could feel my heart stopping and starting again, and I rang for the nurse. She immediately summoned for assistance and said she would notify Marie as I was in serious trouble. I said, "If I am not going to make it, please let Marie sleep and don't call until it is over. I didn't want her to see it happen." Everything went black, and that was all I remembered until Marie came in the morning and let me know her displeasure of not being made aware of the crisis during the night.

On Sunday, June 17, as I approached Val's room, I noticed a nurse sitting outside his room with the Venetian blinds drawn up to allow her to look into Val's room to observe him closely. This was an unusual procedure to have this kind of observation on a patient. The blinds were usually drawn closed unless there was a problem. The nurse said to me, "Before you go in, you should know we had a code blue on your husband last night and came close to losing him. We wanted to call you, but he asked us not to disturb you and let you sleep."

The nurse entered the room with me and listened as I chastised Val. I said to him, "It's not fair for you to decide for me if I should be with you. I would have at least wanted to hold your hand." I added, "It's not right for you to take that away from me. We have a commitment to one another for better or worse, until death do us part. Just think if the situation was reversed, me here instead of you. What would

be your reaction, and what would you have wanted to do?"
Val assured me that it would never happen again if a similar
situation occurred.

PLACED ON THE LIST, BUT ...

Dr. Eastburn, the cardiologist, came to see him at 9:30 a.m. and said to Val, "How are you, buddy?"

Val answered, "I'm still here."

Dr. Eastburn told him, "Today you are being placed on the list for a transplant."

Val asked, "What about all the tests to make sure I can handle a transplant?"

Dr. Eastburn replied, "They are all done. We just have to wait for an organ to become available. You will remain in the hospital until you get the heart transplant or until you die."

In the days that followed, we went about things as normally as we possibly could given the situation we were in. Val kept his mind occupied with his project, and I was in and out, up and down, and all around. I kept myself busy. I went to the cafeteria, ventured outside for walks, went to lunch, spent a lot of time in the chapel, and never stayed away from Val for very long. I simply took short jaunts here and there. For me, I took comfort in seeking out people who needed consolation. I also spent many hours in prayer at Rhea Chapel. I could not have survived without this prayer time, for every waking moment was an anxious waiting game. That was the most difficult part of the whole ordeal. Each time the door opened in Val's room, my heart started to pound, and immediately I wondered if there was encouraging news about an available donor heart. It was a helpless situation.

One day, I was on my way to the cafeteria, and I noticed a woman who looked like she was choking on her own tears. Her emotional strain was very visible, so I approached her and put my arms around her and asked her if she was all right. She shook her head no and leaned up against the wall. I was at a loss for words but did manage to ask her if I could say a prayer. She nodded. I hugged her tightly as I prayed. When I finished, she told me, "My thirteen-year-old son just shot himself. He is not expected to make it." I could not imagine myself in her shoes. At that point, some friends joined her, so I continued to the cafeteria.

As I returned from the cafeteria, I realized some thirteen-year-olds are the same size as Val. I began to agonize as I felt a heavy burden come down on me. As much as I loved Val, I found myself praying for the young boy who might not get the chance to live and grow up and for the pain his mother was going through. It was rough.

An escort service was available at the hotel that I relocated to earlier in the day. I was given a set of instructions to see the receptionist in the main lobby of the hospital in order to get the telephone number of the escort who would see me safely to my hotel at night.

I was going down in the elevator when a woman I befriended leaned in close to me and ever so softly whispered to me, "That girl standing next to you just lost her brother in an accident. He was twenty-two, and his family donated all his organs. Maybe this is a chance for your husband." The girl next to me was crying. I touched her hand just to let her know I felt sad for her. There were no words exchanged or eye contact made. When we got off the elevator, the girl joined a group of about thirty people in the lobby.

I went to the reception desk to get the escort's telephone number. The receptionist wrote the number down, and just as the telephone number was being handed to me, there was a blood-curdling scream coming from the middle of the group where the young girl was who had just lost her brother. I gasped, threw my arms up in the air, my eyes widened, and I stood there frozen. I could not move. The receptionist grabbed my arm and said, "It goes right through you, doesn't it?" I felt like the scream had pierced my soul. I replied, "Yes, especially when your husband is on the heart transplant list."

She said, "Oh, my God!"

I took the telephone number from her and side-stepped in order to avoid any eye contact with the grieving people. I walked straight ahead to the elevator.

Once inside the elevator, I was relieved to be alone. I lost control and began to cry so hard and wondered at the same time, *How will I ever be able to go through with Val getting a heart transplant knowing the pain and the loss others must endure?* Seeing the two families that day had just devastated me.

I went to one of the nurses in the critical care unit (in a different wing than Val was in), and I explained what had just happened, and she held me, and I sobbed. Her suggestion to me was to make an appointment with the social worker. After a restless night, I spent three hours with the social worker. She said the experiences I had gone through the previous day were highly unusual because rarely would a potential recipient family ever come in contact with a donor family. The social worker was able to help me understand and deal with the feelings I was experiencing. I felt consoled and ready for whatever happened even to the point of realizing Val may not ever receive a heart transplant.

It was Saturday, June 30, when things began to happen that would create some havoc—havoc for both of us. Val was a patient of two doctors since the time he was admitted to the hospital and had grown close to and felt secure in their care. Late on Saturday evening, Val was visited by these two doctors and was asked, "Do you know what tomorrow is?"

Val replied, excitedly, "I'm going to get a heart."

They said, "No, not even close; you're getting our replacements."

Val said, "What do you mean?"

They answered, "On the first of every month, we rotate to a different area of the hospital." This was unknown to us until then, and it came as a shock to Val and me.

On Sunday, July 1, since Val was so secure with the doctors who were following his case, it was difficult for him when the newly assigned doctors presented themselves. They were the total opposite of what Val had become accustomed to. On July 2, Monday, one of those doctors bounced into the room, took a hold of Val's IV pole, and proudly stated, "Mr. Bouchard! We're going to get you off these IV drips and get you home with a beeper." I was sitting in a chair, shocked at what this doctor was saying, and I thought to myself, *This can't be happening.* To add even more excitement to the scenario, a nurse came into the room and confirmed this. I felt like someone just shot me at point-blank range and made a bull's-eye on my forehead right between the eyes. I had hoped there would be no more obstacles put in our way. I wanted so desperately not to give up and to hang in there, for my spiritual strength was beginning to wane.

Tuesday, July 3, Val's cardiologist came to the room. We had not seen him in a couple of days. We were anxious to have him clarify what we had been led to believe for the past two days. We immediately were being told exactly what we did not want to hear, confirmation that he was being released to go home and to carry a beeper. Dr. Eastburn said it this way: "Tentatively, toward the end of the week, you will be discharged, and you may go home on a beeper." I felt let down and began to cry because I was led to believe that we would remain in the hospital until the final answer came.

Dr. Eastburn asked me, "What's the matter?"

I replied, "I see what you don't see, and I see it even before you see it."

He replied, "What the heck kind of talk is that?"

I explained, "I know you have fine-tuned Val, but now I have a problem with me, Dr. Eastburn, and not with you."

He asked me, "What kind of problem are you talking about?"

I answered, "Well, Val is starting to get into trouble now, and I can see this happening. Yeah, he looks great, but he is starting to have fluid retention. I know it's not noticeable to you yet, but I have always been able to tell."

He said, "Well, you can always bring him back."

I said, "Wow. That is easy for you to say, but not easy for me to do. And if a problem arises, I have to drive three hours back with a time bomb. I understand your hands are tied because Val can now take oral medications rather than intravenously and there really isn't a choice. It is just so disappointing, and I know you understand. We sincerely appreciate the care Val has received because he is going home, looking better than when we came here. *It was our hope.*"

Dr. Eastburn looked at me, turned, and walked out with the nurse. I could see the tears in her eyes and knew there was not anything the doctor could do about the situation we were in. I realized Dr. Eastburn felt bad.

Val was especially looking forward to meeting Dr. Frist from the first day he arrived at Vanderbilt. Every evening he looked like a disappointed little boy because he didn't get to see Dr. Frist, and it crushed him. I cried a lot that day on Tuesday the third. I clicked my heels up and down the hallway going to Rhea Chapel, where I spent a big portion of my day. Moreover, I clicked them rather loudly. Val said he could not understand why I was crying so much, that he was happy to be going home. He said he would rather wait at home than wait at the hospital. I thought to myself, *How could he be so hardhearted?* This man, who could never stand to see me cry, now suddenly he could not understand why

I was not just crying but bawling and offered no comfort. Just that he wanted to go home and wait. Every time he asked me why I was crying, I would click some more down the hallway to the chapel and then back. I was in and out of conferences with God in Rhea Chapel all day long. "Lord," I said, "I know I have not taken this very well. I am resisting going to Oak Ridge, for I do not want to go back there. I am tired. I gave Val up to you twice in Oak Ridge, and you gave him back to me. I am indeed thankful for the extra time; it has been a bonus. I can understand if you want me to be with him if he dies. I just want you to send us anywhere but back home. I do not want to deal with friends or family. I have not dealt with what happened on the tenth of June. How will I ever to be able to cope with watching him walk up and down the stairs? He refused before to let us set up a bed in our family room downstairs, insisting on sleeping in our own bedroom upstairs."

At 7:00 p.m., I was completely exhausted, and I told Val I just wanted to go to the hotel and go to bed. He understood, and he did not have a problem with me leaving, for he said, "You do look exhausted." He was being kind. He should have said I looked like hell. My last thoughts before I drifted off to sleep were, *Do not let your hearts be troubled. Trust in God still and trust in me*" (John 14:1).

Wednesday, July 4. I usually got to the hospital around 7:00 a.m., but this day was different. It was almost 9:00 a.m. I forced myself to walk through the doors at Vanderbilt. It was a struggle, and for some reason, I was not looking forward to facing the day. As I approached Val's room, I could see him standing in the doorway talking to the wife of a heart transplant patient. Just about the time I approached Val's room, I heard Ann say to Val, "When you come back next week, Val." That was all I needed to hear. I had not even had the chance to say hello yet. So, upon hearing what I heard, I blurted out, "I'm going to the chapel." Val gave a giggle and said, "There she goes to do her thing."

My heels did not just click down the hall; now they stomped loudly down the hall. I did not stay in the chapel very long, but I said prayerfully, "Lord, I don't know what you have planned for me today, but I cannot stay in here all day and hide. I may as well go face whatever it is you have planned."

Val was sitting on the bed when I walked into his room. He looked at me and said, "I have been discharged."

I said, "I thought so with what I heard Ann say."

I let our son Val know we would be home sometime late in the afternoon. I had not had a chance to talk to Jim; however, he called us at the hospital to say he and his family would be out for the day. I told him, "You may call us at home tonight; your father has been discharged."

He asked, "How come you are going home?"

"That's just the way it is."

"You do not sound happy about this decision."

"You got it."

"It sounds like you can't talk."

"You're right. Give my love to Valarie and kiss Bethany for us." We said good-bye.

I told Val, "It's a beautiful day outside, but it is going to be very hot. I have many things to do before we leave, so I will be back for you in about an hour." He asked me what would take so long. I said, "For one thing, it is a long walk to where I keep the car parked. Vanderbilt provides a free parking space quite a distance from the hospital. During the week, a shuttle bus is available and provides transportation from the parking lot to the hospital. On holidays and weekends it's not available, and today my feet will take me to my car."

As I went outdoors and started the long walk to the car, my only thought was how hot it was. My feet were burning from the hot sidewalk. My thin leather-soled shoes were not much protection. My hair was falling in my face because my head was sweating, and sweat was dripping down my face. By the time I reached my car, I was soaked. As I looked at the car, I wanted to turn and run away.

I had parked the car under a big tree so it would not be in the sun. This turned out to be a big mistake. It was covered with dried-up fallen leaves and bird droppings. It had been a few weeks since I had checked on the car since everything I had needed was within walking distance. I had not even left the windows cracked, so when I opened the car door, it felt like an oven. To boot, I needed gas and windshield washer fluid. I did not know which direction to go, so I just drove until I found a gas station. It was not long before I found one. I filled the car with gas and windshield washer fluid. I got a free car wash with the fill-up. It was the first really nice thing that happened to me in a while. After the car was cleaned up, inside and out, I felt ready to take Val home.

I went to the hotel to check out. My clothes were already packed in the room, but I couldn't find a parking place without having to pay to park, and I was not about to pay for parking just to put my clothes in the car to go home. I decided to pick up Val at the hospital and return to the hotel. I could double park with Val staying in the car, and I could pick up my clothes. It was 12:15 p.m. When I asked Val if he was ready to leave, he said, "I just want to meet Dr. Frist before we go home."

I asked him, "Is he supposed to come? We have been here for three weeks now, and you have been told he was going to come visit you. When he did not come, I shared in your disappointments. Emotionally, I do not think I can take your being disappointed again. On a personal note, I do not care if I ever meet him. He is a very busy man, and I am sure there are good reasons why he has not been to see you. I feel the important thing is that Dr. Frist does the surgery if the time comes."

Val said, "Well, it's very important to me."

"Tell you what," I replied. "I am going to the chapel one more time. When I return, have a definite answer if he is going to see you or not."

As I knelt in Rhea Chapel to pray, I said, "Lord, I feel like I have gone through a crucifixion myself the past few days. It is not going to be easy for me to take Val home. I totally surrender and abandon myself to you again. I put my trust in you, for you must carry me all the way now. I will put my time bomb on the seat next to me, and you will have to drive the car, for I have nothing left to give. I have given you my all."

DR. FRIST

I arrived back in Val's room at 12:30 p.m. Val said, "Dr. Frist will be here at 2:00 p.m."

I said, "Fine, but can we have an agreement? If he doesn't come by 3:00 p.m., we will leave. I don't want to drive when it gets dark, and we have to keep in mind it is the Fourth of July and traffic may be heavy."

Neither one of us knows what happened between twelve thirty and two. It seemed to have spanned only minutes in between, and the door opened and in walked this handsome man in such a gentle manner. He said, "Hello, I'm Dr. Frist."

Val smiled—no he beamed—and said, "I'm so happy I finally get to meet you." Dr. Frist sat in a chair next to the bed, and I was standing near a window leaning against the walls with my arms behind me and my hands bracing the wall supporting me.

Dr. Frist asked Val, "What do you think about this transplant business?"

Val said, "It's better than the alternative. Without it, I'll die. My pump is just all worn out." Val also mentioned to Dr. Frist he'd read his book about three or four times.

Dr. Frist asked Val, "So, what did you think about the book?"

Val answered him, "I agreed with your father. I would

not have given you a monkey either." Val never lost his sense of humor.

When I heard Val and Dr. Frist laugh, I wondered as I looked out the window at the blue sky and white clouds and thought, *How can he be so humorous at a time like this. I can't even force a smile, let alone laugh.*

Dr. Frist turned to look at me, and before he had a chance to say anything to me, I said, "I know I look terrible. I've been bounced off the wall one time too many and sure have been crying a lot."

Dr. Frist said, "With a transplant, you will be bounced off the wall a lot."

I said, "We informed ourselves and took advantage of all the information that was available to us about transplantation. I was prepared for the heavy-duty ups and downs we would face; what I was not prepared for was the unnecessary stress that I could have done without. Things like, 'you will stay here until you get a heart or die.' Then all of a sudden the news comes that you are going home in a few days. Feelings of despair and panic set off an emotional switch. I soon came to terms with reality and knew I would have to get prepared for Val and me to go home.

"Since Dr. Eastburn said it would be tentatively toward the end of the week on Tuesday, I thought I had a few days to adjust and be emotionally ready to take him home. If we were lucky, the end of the week might be Friday or Saturday. I was not expecting a time bomb dropped in my lap today when I came to visit Val and to find out he was being discharged. I am not complaining. Val looks great. The care he has received has been excellent. As far as I am concerned, he has been fine-tuned by the best. Who could ask for anything more? It's still difficult to say the least. I am a survivor and will do whatever I need to do."

Dr. Frist turned to Val and said, "What if I told you that you aren't going anywhere and I would like for you to stick around for a few days?"

"Then I would stay."

Oh God, thank you. I do not have to take him home today. I started to sweat, my knees were shaking, and I felt like I was going to fall, so I steadied myself by pushing my hands harder against the wall. I wanted to shout at the top of my lungs for joy at how I was feeling at that moment.

Dr. Frist then said, "How about three or four days?"

Val answered, "I was in the military for twenty years, and I didn't have a choice of when or where I wanted to go or come back. I did what I was told."

Dr. Frist stunned us both with his next statement. "And what if I told you I was going to get a heart for you tonight?" Seldom is Val ever at a loss for words, but he was now. Dr. Frist stood up and said, "You have four hours together." I asked Dr. Frist if Val and I could take a few minutes to go to Rhea Chapel. He said, "You have fifteen minutes." As he walked out the door, Dr. Frist shocked the nurses by saying, "Holly, I think I'll transplant Mr. Bouchard tonight."

"Well, well, yes. Okay, Dr. Frist, I'll get started right away."

Val and I walked hand in hand to the chapel. We prayed together, and then we had our own silent prayer.

To God, I said, "Lord, you never cease to amaze me for you have taken us to the razor's edge. You have taken a tornado and replaced it with a rainbow. We have been on trial for six years; now the trial is over. You have given us your answer. Thank you for saying yes. I hope we never disappoint you and remain worthy of the precious gift Val is about to receive."

When we got back from Rhea Chapel, everything was in place to start preparing Val with IV medications. It was an exciting atmosphere as the word traveled about Val receiving the gift of life. Many came to wish him well; everyone was happy for both of us.

I notified our son Val that we would not be coming home but rather his father was now scheduled to undergo the heart-transplant surgery. I also asked him to leave word with his brother in Connecticut on his answering machine. Then I called our friends Barbara and John, and they were delighted to come and be with me during the time Val would be in surgery.

At 3:15 p.m., Dr. Eastburn, the cardiologist, called me and said, "Mrs. Bouchard, this is Dr. Eastburn. I'm so sorry. I'm sorry. I'm so sorry. Honest to God, I did not know." By that, I assumed he meant he was unaware of the availability of the heart.

I replied to Dr. Eastburn, "There is no need for you to say you're sorry because we are where we need to be. This was our hope, and hope has come."

The way everything transpired was so unusual, even in these circumstances. To me, this helps illustrate the emotional response of physicians in this area of the medical profession. The need for the doctors to remain somewhat unattached is unavoidable; however, it is not true in all cases. It seemed evident to me in this case there was an element of strain for Dr. Eastburn not necessary in my mind. I understand doctors must do what they feel is the right thing, at any given time, and to do so in a way as to avoid burnout.

Barbara and John arrived, and they were able to visit Val for only a short time. At 6:00 p.m., I was invited to go with Val as far as the elevator.

Marie and I went to the chapel for a thanksgiving for life. When we returned, the room had IV stands with solutions hanging on them. I do not know what they all were for, but some were antirejection medications for the new heart, some were antibiotics, blood plasma, and some others.

The IVs were started immediately, and we were told I would be going to the operating room at 6:00 p.m. Time went by fast, and during this time, many of the patients waiting for a transplant and their spouses came and congratulated us. Tears of happiness were shed by the spouses. I believe this gave them hope. Some of those waiting had the look *I wish it were me* but were happy for us. When I saw this, I hoped that many organs could arrive and save my dear friends. As six o'clock approached, I was anxious, and Holly came back with an injection to help me to relax. In a few minutes, a gurney with two attendants arrived, and this was it.

Marie and I had a minute together, and much was thought, and little was said. Many of the hospital staff in the ICCU and step down units were in the hall wishing us the best. At the elevator, I entered and Marie had to stay behind. Down four floors and down a hallway, they parked me outside the operating room. The nurse came out and said it would be one minute and they would bring me on in.

What does one do in the hall waiting to enter for a life-saving operation? I counted the ceiling tiles and tried to estimate how many there were. My mind drifted to the chances for real success. Twenty-five percent of transplants did not make it off the operating table, but I would since I was ready and everyone was praying for us. The good Lord would hear the prayers. I was not worried, nervous, or uptight. They came for me, and again I hoped for victory over the shadow. I was shifted onto the operating table, and suddenly I felt alone. They introduced themselves to me; however, I did not know who was who as they all had masks. Someone talked to me most of the time.

Dr. Frist's assistant explained what would occur. Dr. Frist was in Atlanta harvesting my heart and would take twenty minutes to fly back to Nashville, allowing fifteen minutes to and from each airport, and exit time would result in a "one from time zero." The heart should be beating within four hours of removal. The net time there would be less than three hours for the implant surgery. Dr. Frist would call as soon as his plane landed.

A semi-tent was placed around my head with the top and back open. The anesthesiologist was behind my head explaining what he would be doing. My left arm was stretched out on an arm rest, and all IVs and monitors were in place. We were just waiting for Dr. Frist's call. The only things that bothered me were the operating tools, and I visualized cutting tools. The nurse came and asked me how I was doing, and she was going to give me something to relax me. I thought to myself, *Why?* as I felt like I was relaxed already. About five seconds after the injection, I started to fade, and I knew this was it and the injection was for real. That is all I remember until someone spoke to me sometime later. Sometime later, I discovered, was 3:00 a.m.

I was on a ventilator, and again I was talked to, and through the blurred vision I saw Marie. It seemed like a very short time, and I guess it was. So it wasn't until late in the morning I awoke in a glass room with a recovery room nurse sitting at the foot of the bed. Surprisingly, the pain was not great at all. I just lay in limbo for a long time. The ventilator was removed Saturday morning, and it was another gagging experience.

I walked alongside the stretcher holding Val's hand, and my thoughts were, *How powerful and magnificent what God has allowed man to achieve.* One word to describe how I felt at that time would be *free*. I was not nervous or scared, and I felt as though the chains that held me bound for the last six years were finally loose. There were no words exchanged between us. I held his hand, and he held mine. We were both very happy. Even with all the turmoil of the previous few days, I still had no anxiety one way or the other. I was at peace. I did not watch the hands of the clock.

I returned to where Barbara and John were waiting for me, and we were brought to the second floor by the hospital staff. The three of us had dinner in the hospital cafeteria, and then we spent some time reading in the waiting area. People who were waiting were all given passes, and for those who needed to stay the night were provided with pillows and blankets.

It was 8:30 p.m. in Nashville, and so it was nine thirty in Connecticut when I telephoned Jim, whom I had not spoken to that day. When Valarie answered the telephone, I said to her, "Dad's about halfway through the surgery." All I could hear at that moment was her response, "What? What? What?" I could also hear Jim in the background say, "What's happened to my dad? Give me the phone." Jim was on the telephone now, so I explained to him what was happening and to have him make some telephone calls for me. I also told him no news was good news. The two of them had not heard any news about the transplant being performed on Val. I had caught them by surprise.

At about 2:00 a.m., Dr. Frist came into the waiting room, and we approached each other. He said to me, in such a kind and gentle way, "Do you have someone with you?" I summoned John and Barbara to come over to where we were standing so they could share with me the information on Val's condition. Dr. Frist said, "The surgery went very well, and he received a good heart. It has taken over very well. You will be able to see him, I would say, in about forty-five minutes. The nurse will call you from the intensive care unit when they have him set up."

We waited for about two hours when the telephone rang and the nurse indicated it would be a little while longer since some new equipment they were using for Val was taking more time to set up. I said, "If you would rather I not visit him until later in the day, it would be all right with me."

She replied, "Oh no, we want you to see him, so just be patient with us for a little while longer."

At 5:15 a.m. we were receiving instructions to put on masks and use a special hand cleanser before we were escorted in to see Val. This was done four times each day, and we would follow the same procedures.

My thought before entering the room was about how perfect the setting was for Val's surgery. Dr. Frist mentions in his book, *Transplant*, the ideal conditions that he prefers when performing surgery. He likes to operate at night. The setting appeared perfect to me; it was peaceful and quiet.

On the Fourth of July, the whole hospital was relatively quiet. As we entered the room to see Val, what I witnessed was beautiful. At first glance, I saw the green line on the monitor clearly illustrating a steady rhythm of his new heart beating, unlike the green lines I used to see zigzag across the monitors just a short time ago. My mind blocked out the many machines he was still connected to, and although he was swollen from surgery, I could not help but notice and be surprised that his body was so warm to the touch. He felt warm, and he was nice and pink in color, not gray like he used to appear. Under the surface of Val's skin, I saw what I could describe as appearing like millions of tiny little butterflies fluttering through his veins almost as they were dancing on top of his skin and all in unison with the beat of the new heart. It was truly beautiful to witness. Dr. Frist explained that it was because he now had a nice new "pump" to pump the blood through his veins and it was so much stronger than the heart he no longer had.

This was indeed a miracle in progress. I saw a different man in appearance than I saw just a short time ago.

After Val was moved from the intensive post operative care unit, we still had to prep and wear a mask each time we visited with him. At that time, Val had to learn all about the medications he must take in order to prevent rejection. Rejection is a possibility with any transplant because the body needs to adjust to the new organ and not fight against it like a foreign object. This is treated with antirejection medications. There is also an attitude change to be dealt with as well, by both Val and me. Transplant recipients, in general, have a tendency to become a little self-centered for a time. I knew how to turn this around quickly because I had gone through this ordeal, as well as him, and I did not want this to interfere with our relationship.

It had been suggested to me at the time of Val's surgery that I take photographs of Val at different times after the surgery because of the rapid changes that would occur. I have pictures of Val after only five days showing how good he looked, and I have other pictures as well. The pictures vividly portray the remarkable differences in Val's appearance as he recovered from the transplant surgery.

I was in this dormant stage for almost three days. Each time Marie came in, she would feel my feet and say how nice and warm they were. Previously my feet were always cold. Saturday night another transplant was to take place, and there was only one transplant recovery room. I had to stay until Monday, so a plastic room was built for the other patient. Monday, another transplant occurred, and it was for Jerry. Marie and I were very happy. Then I was moved to the step down unit to continue to recover and would remain there until discharge and live adjacent to the Vanderbilt Medical Center until final release. I did well and had no heart rejection.

I started back on my waste project in a few days. Part of the antirejection medication was Prednisone, a steroid. The high dosage of this drug kept me awake essentially twenty-four hours a day, so I worked on the project around the clock for days and days. When I told Dr. Eastburn I did not sleep the day before, he would say, "Don't worry about it." Marie, my angel, was looking good again. She was eating and resting both mentally and physically. We could not kiss because she wore a mask over her face, but we were able to hug.

I was asked to take pictures of myself, and I asked why—to see if I changed over time. One day I looked at myself in the mirror and then at a picture, and lo and behold, I had a fat face. My hair grew a half an inch a week, so if I didn't comb it, I looked like a wild man. My beard grew long every day. Some patients, especially women, grow facial hair and hairy arms. Some children's eyebrows grow bushy, and their eyelashes grow long. I was required to walk around the unit floor many times for exercise. I was to decrease from three hundred milligrams of Prednisone to ten milligrams every week for ten weeks, then five milligrams per week for twenty weeks, and then finally went off Prednisone after six years. I did not enjoy my facial look or weight gain, but what choice did I have?

Marie had moved from the hotel to an apartment in

the Village at Vanderbilt, which was across the street from the hospital. She made preparations for my discharge. She said we would never survive in one room for months as the Prednisone made my mind change and I did many strange things. I could close my eyes and think what would the room look like, blue or red or yellow, and the room color would change. I would be talking to someone on the phone and forget who I was talking to. Later when Marie drove, I would say, "You are following too close, too far back, go in the left lane, go in the right lane." After I would say all that, I wondered why I'd said it. I always had a comment, which, before, I did not comment. How much longer on the steroids? It's a wonder she did not lose her patience with me.

I was discharged from the hospital on the twelfth day after my transplant and to begin the exercise and medical program for final discharge. In my life, I never had time to exercise and should have made the time. I used the treadmill, steps, rowing machine, and walked. When I left the hospital and went outside, I cried tears of overwhelming joy, and all I could think was, *Thank you, Lord!*

Five days after surgery

Ten days

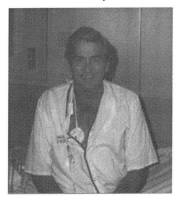

Fifteen days

The fifteenth of July was the day I rented an apartment at The Village at Vanderbilt. On July 16, Val was discharged from the hospital to live with me in the apartment. It was an extremely emotional day for him, and he started to cry. Val had been very near death when he was admitted just a little more than a month before. Now, he was being discharged with a new life, leaving the sense of security he had gained by being in the hospital.

The first day of our new routine would include a follow-up at the clinic. On our very first visit to the clinic, Dr. Eastburn, the cardiologist, made a comment to another doctor upon seeing us: "The way this guy got his heart, you could not have written a better television script." When I heard this, I immediately thought in my mind, *Gee, people have been telling us to write a book about this miracle.* So I had to ask myself again, *What is it God is trying to tell me? Where could this possibly go?*

On Val's sixty-second birthday, August 13, his sister Elaine came to visit. We went to the arboretum at the Grand Ole Opry Hotel in Nashville. I watched Val walk with his sister along a path in the arboretum, as I had dropped back behind them, and I noticed him bend down, cup the petals of a pansy flower delicately with the fingers of his hand. A month ago, this man struggled to tie his shoes, and here he was, effortlessly bending over to look at a flower. He studied it as if it was a rare find, and I was in awe to think this man was so near death a short time ago. He would also reach up and caress the leaves of the trees as he walked by them. He took careful consideration of the nature around him as if for the very first time. He was so engrossed in everything around him he did not notice I was not walking alongside them until he came to some stairs that led to a landing overlooking the entire arboretum.

After Val ascended just three steps, he stopped and looked around, searching for me, and when our eyes met, I asked, "You are not going to go up all those stairs, are you?"

"Yes, why not?" he replied.

"Yes, why not?" I answered.

"What's the matter? You do not seem happy."

"I'm happy. You just would not understand. What I am seeing is not what you see. This is so much more than I could have ever dreamed of."

One evening, I was taken by surprise when the manager of the Village Apartments telephoned me to tell me she had met the nurse who accompanied Dr. Frist when he retrieved Val's heart. Arrangements were made for her and her boyfriend to come visit with Val and me at our apartment. The girl was a medical student at Vanderbilt, and she wanted to tell me about the day she went with Dr. Frist. It was at a point when she was contemplating her future.

She was getting ready to go out when she received the telephone call on July 4 and was invited to go with Dr. Frist to retrieve a heart. She told us about going to the airport in the racing ambulance with the sirens sounding. The doors opened rapidly; they jumped out and ran to a waiting jet all ready to take off. The jet propelled straight up into the sky while her stomach was left back on the ground where the ambulance stopped. When the jet landed, they were met with a waiting ambulance. They took their igloo cooler and were whisked off to the hospital to retrieve the organ.

Upon arrival at the hospital, the ambulance and hospital doors were held open for them to run through. There were different teams ready, and a strategy was in place for the organ retrieval process. The utmost respect was awarded to the donor throughout the entire process. As soon as the organ was placed inside the igloo cooler, they ran as fast as they could back to the waiting ambulance, racing past the open doors into the ambulance and whisked off to the waiting jet ready to transport them back to the university. In the meantime, the hospital was notified that the surgery was a "go." The recipient was then prepared for the surgery. She also told me that she had been permitted to stand behind the anesthesiologist and watch the surgery in its entirety. This, she told us, forever changed her life. It gave her the determination to continue medical school.

As the time grew near to when we left the apartment and Nashville to return home to Oak Ridge, I could not help but think to myself how much I wished we could stay a little longer. It was like a honeymoon that I did not want to end. It was like going back six years prior to Val's first heart attack and picking up from there. Not only did Val receive a new heart, we also had the gift of an intimate relationship again, so what more could I ask? Well, maybe, as Garth Brooks sings, "I could have missed the dance." So, I still have that to look forward to. Thank you, Lord, for our eyes have witnessed the glory of how powerful your divine intervention had been.

Dr. Frist, Val and Marie

LAST WISH

Val with granddaughter, Mariealaina

Summer 2006 - During the summer Val was getting very tired. He continued to cut the grass with a riding lawn mower. He got to the point of having to sit on the ground while gardening and would have the grandchildren help and work with him digging the holes for the flowers that Val so loved. He loved to work in the yard. Val could still drive, so he drove himself to the store for all the purchases and planned all the gardening work, both at home and at the Angel Garden.

After each area of the yard was weeded, prepared, and the flowers planted, Val would come to see me and ask,

"Do you like the flowers?" I would reply, "Yes, what's not to like?" To myself I thought how it really broke my heart to see and watch Val give so much of himself for me and all I could do was pray a lot in order to endure.

Val grew more tired and rested more frequently. In July, when Val received a notice of his sixtieth high school reunion to take place in September at Adams, Massachusetts, I told him that I would send a response that he was not able to attend. However, over the next few weeks, we received telephone calls from his classmates asking if we would be there in September. Early September, Val asked me if I would please take him to the reunion. This meant a one-thousand-mile trip in the car, and I said no. A week later, Val asked me again, and I said no again. A few days later, Val asked me again, "Marie, won't you please reconsider and take me to the reunion? It's important to me."

I thought to myself for just a second and replied to Val, "We have never had to beg each other for anything, and you don't have to start now. If it's all right with you, I will make arrangements with Dr. McLaughlin and let him make the decision if he feels you can make the trip or not." Val agreed and told me that would be fine.

Dr. McLaughlin said to Val, "You have been through a lot, and I think this is just what you need, so go with my blessings, and I will want to see you as soon as you return."

We arrived at Val's brother George's house on September 22 and attended the reunion together on the twenty-third. Val spoke to the class, saying good-bye. It was so painful for me as I knew in my heart what he was doing, but no one else could see what I was witnessing.

They had no idea Val was so ill. He had an amazing ability to pull himself up so that people couldn't see how sick he really was. Val's brother and I knew he was ready to go home to Oak Ridge on the Monday, the twenty-fifth, following the reunion.

Last photo with brother George, Sept. 23, 2006

Class Reunion

We made an appointment with Dr. McLaughlin, and Val spent a few days in the hospital. When he came home, he mostly rested on the couch, lying with his eyes closed. This broke my heart because we both knew, but we remained silent. I knew that Val couldn't look at me because he could see my pain even though I kept myself pretty and tried to keep a smile on my face.

We had a doctor's appointment around September 30, and when the doctor examined Val, while he sat in a wheelchair, the doctor looked at me, shaking his head with grave disappointment. The doctor approached me and said, "When the time comes, you will get all the support you need." Val was looking at me, and so I smiled at the doctor so Val would not be able to pick up on my expression and figure out what the doctor was telling me. I was not expecting to hear what the doctor said that day. When we were ready to leave the doctor's office, he assured me with these words out of earshot of Val: "You will know when and you can call me and I will make all the arrangements for hospice." I guess Val knew, but we never did talk about what it was Dr. McLaughlin said to me.

Sunday, October 15, Val came downstairs for the last time with the help of our granddaughter. I did not want him to come downstairs, but he did anyway. That evening our son, grandson, and daughter-in-law all helped to get Val upstairs to our bedroom. It was pitiful to see him struggle. The next day the sisters from St. Mary's came to see Val and thanked him for all his involvement in the community. He held their hands and thanked them for coming to see him. Anyone could have seen right away the joy on his face at seeing them. A few of the Knights of Columbus also came, but Val was very tired and didn't say much. On Tuesday, the seventeenth, I called the doctor and told him it was time, and hospice came. Thursday, a nurse came and gave Val a bath, and I took care of him over the weekend. I never left his side unless someone was with him. On the nineteenth, hospice returned and bathed him again. Our priest came and spent a few hours on the twenty-first. Hospice returned on Tuesday and Thursday, and his caretaker told me Val was all worn out, but he was able to do all the things she asked him to do. In other words, he was doing what he could to help her. He was lying on his back, propped up on pillows with his hands crossed. His face was pointed up to the ceiling and had what appeared to be a look of strain and pain. Up to this time, Val had not taken or asked for any pain medication. Through Val's feeding tube, I gave him pain medication, and he seemed to rest more comfortably.

On Friday, October 27, Val began to have labored breathing, but he was also nice and warm, and his face had good color, pink. He had been warm for a few days. My friend who is a nurse was with me Sunday. She and my granddaughter were going to lift Val up higher on the bed pillows when he stopped breathing. I ran downstairs to call hospice when my granddaughter called to me saying, "Papa is breathing again." This occurred three times that day, and Val continued with labored breathing.

Jim, his wife, and our grandchildren came by that evening after they returned from having been out of town over the weekend to see me and their father and grandfather. As

I got myself ready for bed, I said to Val, "Honey, my little legs are very cold tonight, so I'm going to warm them with your legs." I still spoke to Val as if he could still hear me even though I wasn't completely sure if he could or not. I took Val's hand, put it on my heart, laid my head on his shoulder, and fell asleep. At 3 a.m., I woke up, sat on the edge of the bed, and said a rosary prayer. Then I turned out the light and got back into the same position as before. At 7 a.m., I woke up again, looked at the clock, and said, "I'm going to see what time Christine has to go to school today." I was surprised when I went to give Val a kiss; his head was turned toward me. I kissed him good morning, got out of bed, and turned to pull the covers up on my side of the bed so that Val wouldn't be uncovered. I then realized he was gone.   Hospice, the priests, and family came to the house. As Val was being taken to the hearse, I walked downstairs and outside behind him each step of the way. I thought to myself, *Rest now, my beloved. You deserve it. You gave your all, and I'm going to miss you.* The funeral was November 4. The Knights of Columbus honor guard was present at both the receiving of friends and at the church funeral service. During the service, Father Woods sang a beautiful rendition of "Eye Is on the Sparrow."

> The Lord is my shepherd; I shall not want. He maketh me to lie down in green pastures: he leadeth me beside the still waters. He restoreth my soul: he leadeth me in the paths of righteousness for his name's sake. Yea, though I walk through the valley of the shadow of death, I will fear no evil: for thou art with me; thy rod and thy staff they comfort me.

Thou preparest a table before me in the presence of mine enemies: thou anointest my head with oil; my cup runneth over. Surely goodness and mercy shall follow me all the days of my life: and I will dwell in the house of the Lord for ever.

Psalm 23:1 (KJV)

Angel Garden, Nov. 4, 2006

REDEEMER OF MYSTERY

The journey will continue in eternal life for Val. The trail of mystery will continue until we meet again. What a glorious reunion it will be.

As I travel the prepared road of mystery, may the hearts who are having difficulty with faith, doubts, frustrations, pain, and self-defeat find love, hope, and peace in the hidden mystery of *Walk with the Shadow*. I will continue to share the experience until my Redeemer calls my name.

Marie E. Bouchard

Vermont wedding, May 11, 1990

EVENTS

1984:

May 30	Heart Attack
July 4	Letter to Val asking for a miracle
July 11	Val flown to UAB

1990:

June 11	Flown to Vanderbilt
July 4	Heart Transplant

2006:

October 30	Passed Away
November 4	Funeral Mass

Memorials to Val:

Donation by the Knights of Columbus to our parish priest Gold Chalice with Val's name and dates inscribed: 8/13/1928; 7/4/1990; 10/30/2006

TRIBUTES

Val occupies a special place within. I have let it be so, and so the miracle goes on. "With the fullness of time, he appeared—the one who wanted to set us free from time." Saint Augustine was referring to Jesus's coming, but I am referring to that "fullness of time" that Val and I shared together.

When we met, it was like meeting someone I had known all my life. We worked and laughed together, and we became brothers in "time." The time we shared together was brief, special, and fulfilling.

Val has been set free from "time" to help do the Lord's work. I, while trapped in "time," will go on in this miracle called life until I too will reach eternity and be with them.

Bobby Lee, a "time" prisoner
Oak Ridge, Tennessee

Val and Marie have documented an incredible journey that started with uncertainty but winds a path through faith, love, and trust. It's nothing short of miraculous.

Thomas F. D'Muhala
Close friend and colleague
Formerly President of the
Shroud of Turin Research Project, Inc.

LIVE

listen|imagine|view|experience

AUDIO BOOK DOWNLOAD INCLUDED WITH THIS BOOK!

In your hands you hold a complete digital entertainment package. In addition to the paper version, you receive a free download of the audio version of this book. Simply use the code listed below when visiting our website. Once downloaded to your computer, you can listen to the book through your computer's speakers, burn it to an audio CD or save the file to your portable music device (such as Apple's popular iPod) and listen on the go!

How to get your free audio book digital download:

1. Visit www.tatepublishing.com and click on the elLIVE logo on the home page.
2. Enter the following coupon code:
   dd06-4ea1-cbc5-1d4d-59ca-0aef-fdf2-2c91
3. Download the audio book from your elLIVE digital locker and begin onjoying your new digital entertainment package today!